MW00880261

Chasing

Grandpa

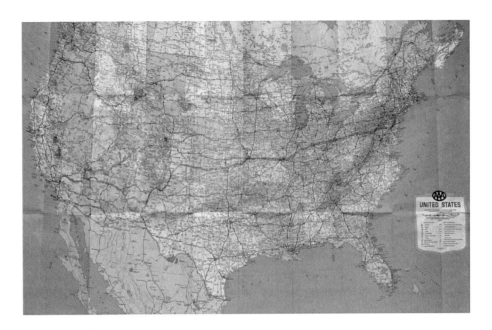

The westward route traveled by C.W. Tuthill and P.G.Scull
in the winter of 1916 to demonstrate the Maxwell Model 25
touring car would make an excellent every day family car.

Chasing Grandpa

By Richard Tuthill Bassemir

No part of this publication may be reproduced in whole or in part, or stored in a retrieval system, or transmitted in any form or in any means, electronic, mechanical, photocopying, recording or otherwise, without the written permission from the author. For information regarding permission email Richard Bassemir at **rbassemir1@gmail.com**

Copyright © 2017 by Richard Tuthill Bassemir

ISBN 978-1-5471-9248-9

Contents

Prologue

It was early morning and the rising sun cast a long misshapen shadow across US 1. At a glance it looked like two gents in frock coats and caps were hunched over the darkened silhouette of a 1917 Maxwell convertible. Rich gave Doug a poke in the ribs and pointed to it. "Look! Grandpa and Scull are following us."

Indeed, as the next week unfolded, it would certainly appear to unbiased eyes as if the two brothers were being guided, inspired and protected either by luck, coincidence or by supernatural forces.

Consider the following:

. . . a man just happens to find a six year old newspaper article about the planned trip and sends an email to Doug just days before they leave with an invitation to provide assistance in the Indianapolis area. This was an offer the boys needed.

. . . a spur-of-the-moment purchase of a tire repair kit for seemingly no reason turns out to come to the rescue three days later.

. . . the Chevy support vehicle develops an intermittent problem while on a deserted road but miraculously manages to keep running to get the boys to their destination.

. . . finding a store open on Thanksgiving day with urgently needed repair parts.

. . . thirteen days on the road with cold but clear weather and only two small rain showers. The only storm that they encountered passed over them while in the warmth of a shop while repairing the Maxwell.

. . . failed radiator fan bearings were replaced with bearings from a damaged radiator fan they just happened to have.

Could the boys just have been extremely lucky or was there someone really watching out for them as they chased Grandpa? You decide.

Acknowledgements

It was just a few days into this trip when John Brasca asked if I planned to write a book about this adventure. My response was almost immediate: "Nope!" I am an engineer and like many engineers, writing was not my strongest skill. As the trip progressed, and we found ourselves in different predicaments, I asked myself if I should write about this. For a month after returning from the adventure I was haunted by the possibility of retelling it.

While attending a Toastmaster meeting and recalling certain events that occurred on the trip Amy Samet, looked at me and said, "You gotta write a book". Amy is an accomplished Toastmaster with a gift for public speaking. I valued her opinion and went home that night thinking, maybe I should try it. The seed was planted.

I had a lot of material to draw from to recount this trip in detail. There were as many as two hundred videos and hundreds of photos. Those photos were all time stamped and included their GPS location thanks to modern technology. That information was helpful for keeping my time and places accurate. I kept a daily log and gathered names and signatures of many folks we met and who had helped us along the way. Of course there was our grandfather's diary but he also left all his grandchildren a four-page typed document about his early years which included a mention of this transcontinental trip.

Over the next few months I plugged away writing and capturing the sequence of events. Starting from the initial idea (which is attributed totally to my brother Doug Bassemir), to a retelling of the actual trip. I even took an audio course on creative writing of non-fiction to improve my writing skills.

Early chapters were only shared with my mother, June Tuthill Bassemir, partly for feedback but also because I knew she would encourage me to continue. Changes were frequent and progress was slow. Thank you, Mom, for all your input. As more of the story was told I started sharing more of the book. Thank you, Doug, in keeping the technical facts accurate and catching lots of inconsistencies.

When I thought I was done, I shared the entire book with Bob Ross, from my local Road Relics Car Club. Bob, I appreciate the time you spent providing great feedback and corrections. After feeling more comfortable with the story I printed off copies and shared them with my sister, Janet Gentile. To say she was helpful would be a gross understatement. Janet spent hours going over the book and finding ways to improve the way the story was told. Janet was also instrumental in the preparation of the many photos used in the book. Thank you so very much Sis.

Again I thought I was done and shared the book proof with my daughter, Casey Bassemir, known to some friends as the, "observer". Her observation skills yielded good feedback. Thank you, Casey for your contributions to the book.

These people helped me nurture the seed and produce a story of this epic tale. This adventure would not have happened without the folks mentioned in the following pages. Their encouragement, financial support, technical expertise, personal time and donations made this trip possible. Without them, this book would not have been possible. Thank you all.

Chapter 1 - Grandpa

Grandpa was a daring and ambitious entrepreneur who would thrust himself into the national spotlight before he was 30. A hundred years later, he would be an inspiration to a new generation; one with more luxuries that he could only dream possible. To his grandsons though, he was no less than the source of a dream, a dream that would educate a generation, and a dream that needed his divine assistance.

Grandpa was born in fall of 1888. This was a time when men labored without the use of heavy machinery, computers, or smart phones. A time when they say men were men. His father, Fred Henry Tuthill and his mother, Ruth Albertson Tuthill were from a long line of Puritan immigrants who settled largely on the east end of Long Island. Grandpa got his start in life in a town called Jamesport. The town provided rich farming land along the Peconic Bay with water passage to the Atlantic Ocean. Grandpa was born at home in a house built in 1730. The house was originally his grandmother's until it was given to his father. Before the railroad was available, the house was an overnight stagecoach stop between Orient Point and Brooklyn. Although the house burnt down many years ago, if you were to drive along Main Street (now called NY 25) through Jamesport, you can see the stone water well on the north side of Main Street just feet from the sidewalk. It is sealed closed now, but it is where Grandpa would fetch water for the house.

C.W. Tuthill's boyhood water well in 1900s and now in 2017

Grandpa's given name was Clifford Wayne Tuthill. He rarely if ever went by the name of Clifford. He much preferred being called Wayne, or CW. However, as he grew into his teens, he adopted the nickname "Tut"; a nickname that matched his rugged personality.

Growing up on the east end of Long Island Grandpa enjoyed what boys typically do at that time. He worked on the farm but being close to the water, he liked "farming" the water. Grandpa would catch eels and crabs in the water ways. At low tide, he would rake for clams in the Peconic Bay and Long Island Sound. He also did seine fishing, which is a method of fishing that uses a long net with weights at the bottom and floats at the top. Two boys would drag the net through the water to catch small bait fish that could be sold to fishermen.

Grandpa was schooled in a one-room school house, but not your typical little red school house. In a letter to his grandchildren, he wrote how it was very elaborate inside and out. His classmates included two Indian children who were, according to Grandpa, very nice. There were also black students in his class of which two of the boys went on to be successful business men in Brooklyn. Grandpa had the same three teachers through the 8th grade. He wrote that when he was too tall to sit in the seats, he went to Riverhead High School that was five miles from home.

For three years, Grandpa traveled back and forth to Riverhead High School. Depending on the weather he would hop on the train, ride a horse and cart, bicycle, or even walk. Grandpa's school work brought him good grades, but he would write that he was too bashful to continue to graduation. Instead, he enrolled in a business school in Jamaica, Long Island, seventy-five miles west of Jamesport. This meant he would have to find room and board in Jamaica while attending school. Unable to find a job to pay his expenses, a month later he was forced to return home to Jamesport.

In 1907, Grandpa turned 18 and started writing about his days in a pocket diary that could easily slip into a shirt or pants pocket. Each daily entry started with the temperature and weather conditions. His hand-written diary entries were brief and told what he did, naming people he met and his observations. For example, he mentions on January 24, 1907 his church was holding a fifteen cent supper, and how in the summer he would pick strawberries and cherries then deliver them by horse and wagon for ten and twelve cents a quart.

Grandpa had a passion for machines and enjoyed tasks that required the use of his hands. His ability to build and fix machines demonstrated he was mechanically astute. In the fall of 1907, he recalls seeing fifty automobiles at the Riverhead County Fair. The automobile industry was flourishing. Grandpa noticed more automobiles and fewer horses and buggies. In the summer of 1908, he used his mechanical skills to land a job at the only auto garage in Riverhead for six dollars a week. He would ride a bicycle five miles back and forth to the garage that summer and fall. Grandpa would write in his diary how he would trap small wild animals for extra money. His diary left it to the reader's imagination what kind of animals he was trapping. They were most likely muskrats.

The summer of 1909, Grandpa found a job that would pay him more. He chauffeured cars for a real estate dealer, Mr. Fishel, in Riverhead, for ten dollars a week. No doubt this was where he picked up knowledge about real estate that would serve him well later in life when he purchased property in Seaford, New York. By the spring of 1910, Grandpa felt he deserved an increase in pay which Mr. Fishel refused to give. Grandpa wrote that he was actually grateful for that because it helped him decide to follow his passion. Grandpa loved machines and did not want to work on a farm because farmers were typically poor in those days. He packed up and found a job in Long Island City in an auto factory making twelve dollars a week. To build his skills the evenings were spent at a night school machine shop class.

A strike at the auto factory in 1911 caused Grandpa to take his skills to the American Locomotive Company, known as Alco. Alco was branching out from locomotives to the automobile industry. The past two years their famous "Black Beast" car had back to back wins at the Vanderbilt Cup Race on Long Island. Grandpa worked for Alco auto factory and was paid twenty-four dollars a week plus expenses. His job took him as far north as Toronto, Canada and as far south as Winston, South Carolina inspecting and repairing automobiles. It was not long before Alco found the automobile business unprofitable for them and abandoned the business in 1913.

When Alco left the automobile business, Grandpa was once again in the job market. He heard of a job opportunity with Thomas A. Edison in West Orange, New Jersey. In February of 1913, he started working for Mr. Edison making twenty-five dollars a week, a dollar more a week than what Alco paid. Grandpa was one of twenty men hired to learn the operation of Edison's motion picture projector that was synchronized with sound. The combination of the motion picture machine with large phonographs was called the kinetophone, later known by the name of Kinetoscope. The era of talking movies had started. Grandpa worked in Edison's lab and saw Mr. Edison and many famous people that came into the lab to see Edison's inventions in operation. After working for Mr. Edison for a year, Grandpa became the chief operator and was sent to Europe to demonstrate the kinetophone. Grandpa thought highly of the Edisons. He attended the same church as Mina Edison and was impressed by her kindness. While Grandpa was suffering from a serious illness, Mina had sent Grandpa a bouquet of flowers wishing him wellness.

In July of 1914, Grandpa was sent on a fourteen-month assignment in Brazil with Raymond A. Linton making a whopping forty-five dollars a week plus expenses. Grandpa wrote that while in Brazil, he visited 45 different cities. When Grandpa's assignment was over, he returned to New York traveling by water. His return trip was through the British West Indies which required him to sail on eighteen different ships, some of which were very small. At 26 he had become a world traveler.

Upon returning to New York in 1915, Grandpa's new assignment was to demonstrate Edison's new motion picture machine. Grandpa traveled across the USA demonstrating this new machine in Dallas, Texas; Atlanta, Georgia; and Nashville, Tennessee. During his travels was when Grandpa took his Aunt Cynthia's advice and sent his first correspondence to Helen Widman, who lived in Newark, New Jersey. It was the start of a courtship that resulted in marriage three years later in 1918.

As the World War 1 clouds were gathering in Europe against Kaiser Wilhelm, Grandpa went to enlist in the Navy. To his disappointment, he was rejected because he was under weight for his six foot two frame. With Edison abandoning his pursuit of the motion picture machine Grandpa found a new job in Newark working for the Ford Motor Company. He worked on the assembly line, a job that was dirty and repetitive. It only took him eighteen days of that type of work to realize this was not for him. He had greater ambitions than to be just a cogwheel in the Ford operations. He was wasting his talents.

In August of 1916, Grandpa landed a much cleaner job. He became a salesman for the Maxwell Motor Corporation in Newark, New Jersey. He was only there a few months when he had an idea to help promote the Maxwell cars. The idea was to drive a Maxwell from the east coast to the west coast and back in the winter months to demonstrate the reliability of the Maxwell touring car. He discussed his idea with another salesman, Percy Scull. Percy agreed to go fifty-fifty with Grandpa. They sold the idea to Texaco and Firestone which would give them the gas, oil, and tires in return for advertising. To further offset their expenses, they obtained donations such as tools, horn, and a spotlight. Since the plan was to do this trip in the winter months, they welcomed a donation of blankets for use on the trip. They bought a demonstration car for $512 that only had 1,500 miles on it.

Grandpa had Texaco and Firestone signage painted on their Maxwell Model 25 and on November 16, 1916 C.W. Tuthill and Percy Scull started on an epic adventure. Grandpa knew this would be a test of not just the Maxwell but a test of skill and determination. What Grandpa did not know was the impact this trip would have on his grandsons.

After marrying Helen Widman in 1918, the couple settled in a small town called Seaford on the south shore of Long Island. The house was on the south side of Merrick Road, the main street of Seaford. Much like his home in Jamesport, the house was close to water. With an eye for property values, he paid to have the water canal dredged thus creating water front property. The canal provided access from the house all the way out to the Great South Bay. A short access road called Tuthill Place was created to provide access to the back of his property and would later be used to build a bungalow. It was in Seaford where he and Helen would raise three boys, one girl. They in turn gave Grandpa and Helen twelve grandchildren.

Raising a family through the great depression was a test of Grandpa's character. He used his talents and entrepreneurial skills to find sources of income and teach the children not to accept defeat. He did not gamble, smoke, or drink because it was a waste of money. On the property, he tended a garden, raised chickens, and owned a cow for milk. Grandpa built a rowboat so the boys could fish in the water ways. Later, he built a larger boat with an inboard motor in the center and a tiller at the stern to steer. This gave him and the boys better access to the bay for fishing and clamming.

C.W. Tuthill with his wife, Helen on the larger boat he built

Grandpa used his business skills to open a restaurant on Merrick road in front of their house. He, Helen, and his mother in-law would run the entire business which became very popular for their fresh clam chowder. In 1933 when prohibition ended he decided to rent out the restaurant because he did not want to serve liquor.

During the depression, Grandpa had an oil delivery business. One evening while going over his records, June, the youngest sibling asked why some of his customers had not paid him. "Because they don't have the money", he would answer.

Grandpa was a member of the Seaford volunteer fire department and a Freemason. He was a role model to his boys, rarely raising his voice or arguing but still taught the boys discipline and how to be creative. As he did when he encouraged the boys to trap muskrats, then skin and sell their pelts. There was the idea to raise money by building a tennis court on the property. That way the boys could maintain it and rent it out. He favored the youngest of the children, the girl June. However he did find it necessary to reprimand her after she said "damn". Even the favored child suffered a spanking. That was the last time she used that word.

June later married and gave Grandpa four grandchildren, two girls, and two boys before he passed away in 1970. The two boys, Rich and Doug have only vague memories of their Grandpa. They knew little about his colorful history. Their only memory was bouncing on Grandpa's knee, but that would change. Grandpa had left a trail of history; it just needed to be discovered.

Chapter 2 – The Discovery

Doug was bent over the driver's side front fender of a 1966 Mustang Coupe studying the engine as it idled with the deep rumble of a race car. The ivory coupe sported a black racing stripe along with Doug's name and blood type painted on the driver's door. The passenger-side door had his navigator Al Rodd's name as well as his blood type. This was one of the many requirements contestants were required to do in order to run in the Mexico's La Carrera Panamericana road race in October 2006. In bold letters on the "C' pillar were the names of Doug's four children and on the deck lid was "Thanks Maria", a tribute to his wife.

Doug was checking the engine out before starting the road trip to Mexico. The plan was for Doug, his engine builder, Tony Bogovich and his partner from the Sheriff's Office, Al Rodd to trailer the Mustang from Long Island to Veracruz, Mexico for the start of the famous Mexico seven-day road race. Along the way, they would stop in Austin, Texas for a quick visit with Doug's brother, Rich, who had recently finished building his own race car, a replica of the 1965 Shelby Cobra. Neither of the boys were professional racers, but both had grown up around cars. Their father taught them the basics about cars. How to repair brakes, change the oil, adjust the points, set the timing of the engine or adjust a carburetor. Many was the time they would work on the lawn mower engine or even repair a lawn mower a neighbor had set out for the trash. The boys learned from their mother who demonstrated restoration skills when she restored a 1931 Model A Sport Coupe. Rich would eventually take possession of his Grandpa's 1955 Buick Special and kept that running as his daily driver while at Virginia Tech. Meanwhile, Doug had a keen eye for cars with potential, frequently buying and sometimes selling cars. The boys did body work, engine work even car painting. Neither one was afraid to disassemble and reassemble any portion of a car that was not working. This was a skill each in their own way carried on beyond the typical teenage years. Perhaps a gene passed on to them by their Grandpa.

Doug tested these skills in the Panamericana race adventure. While Doug and his team did not win, they did finish the seven-day race. For first-time participants, that was a feat not to be taken lightly. Following the Panamericana Doug kept the Mustang, taking it to an occasional car show where it would proudly display the La Carrera Panamericana logo with the number 351. Doug would retell his experience with that race to many car enthusiasts. It was after that Panamericana race that Doug stumbled across what would become the next adventure.

Doug was on his way to visit his mother just a few miles away from his own house to help her with some chores. She was doing spring cleaning and needed some muscle to move boxes from the attic down a flight of steps to the living room for inspection. When Doug arrived, the garage door was open. He squeezed between the cars in the garage and made his way up the steps into the house. As he opened the door, the familiar aroma of home cooking filled the air. On the stove just inside the door, a pot of clam chowder was simmering. Not just any clam chowder, on the stove was a pot of Tuthill Clam Chowder from a recipe that had been passed down through the ages. This recipe made the Tuthill Restaurant in Seaford a favorite spot for lunch in the 1930s. The smell filled the kitchen and made Doug's mouth water. A bowl of soup would be a welcome reward for helping his mother around the house.

Doug hugged his mother and quickly headed upstairs to the attic to bring down several boxes. His time was precious and the sooner he finished the sooner he could return home for his own chores. His mother already started sorting out papers and photos across the dining room table. Doug sat down a shoe box of photos on the table when an old news clipping caught his attention. The headlines read:

"TOURING COUNTRY IN MAXWELL CAR ARE THESE TWO"

It was an article from a January 1917 issue of the New Orleans Times-Picayune. The article included a picture of two men standing next to a Maxwell covered in mud and dirt, but the Texaco and Firestone signage was clearly visible on the doors. Two other men were sitting in the Maxwell. The caption under the photo identified the driver as none other than C.W. Tuthill and the passenger was P.G. Scull.

Doug, with his deep fascination of old cars, read the article with extreme interest. The article talked about the route Tuthill, and Scull had taken from Newark, New Jersey, through Pittsburgh, Indianapolis, Kansas City, Lamar, Santa Fe, Needles, and ultimately Los Angeles. After a short stay and visits to San Francisco and San Diego, the two returned on a southern route. The two traveled through Tucson, Dallas, New Orleans, Charlotte, Richmond,

Philadelphia, and finally returned to Newark. When he set the article back on the table the questions started to flow. Doug wanted to know what his mother knew about the trip. Did Grandpa ever discuss it with her? What happened to the car? Doug had many questions, that his mother could not answer, but she knew where to get the answers. Among the boxes was a rather flat box that looked like it might have held a photo album in a prior life.

Lifting the top off the box revealed twelve pocket size note books. They were not all identical, but each had well worn edges and corners. Each was held closed with a strap. They were the yearly journals that Grandpa had kept from 1907 to 1919. Each one had a day by day chronology in the life of C.W. Tuthill. The hand-written entries started with the day's temperature and weather followed by comments about the day's events. It was like going back in time. A door had been opened to the past.

Doug pulled out the journal for 1916 and looked for mention of the November cross-country trip. Excitedly Doug read the following entry for November 14, 1916.

Nov. 14, 1916 Therm 70-50, Weather partly cloudy. Went over to NY again in the PM. We bought the car today for $512 and are going tomorrow or Thurs. Met H. Took her for a ride. Left her my r.

His mother helped interpret the short hand. When he mentions "H" that was Helen Widman and left her my "r" was his ring. Grandpa would marry Helen two years later.

In the back of the 1916 journal was a hidden compartment. Tucked in that compartment was the Lord Motor Car Co. business card belonging to F.L. Chavanne, identifying a Maxwell dealership address on Eleventh and Hope, Los Angeles, California. Apparently one of the dealers Grandpa had met with on the trip.

Business card found in the diary

Also in the hidden compartment was a neatly folded newspaper clipping of a Texaco ad. It read "Through the Rockies in November"

Article hidden at the back of the diary

With a little more digging through the spring cleaning boxes, another discovery was made. It was an envelope yellowed with age containing pictures taken by Grandpa while on the cross-country trip. Each photo had hand written notes on the back revealing the location of the picture. There were pictures of them in the mud in Ohio, the ferry in Missouri, outside a hotel in Lamar, Colorado and in the Mojave Desert. The 90-year-old pictures were faded but in surprisingly good condition for their age.

In the same box with the old photos was a second envelope. In it were letters and postcards Grandpa had sent while on his adventure to Helen Widman. Some letters were hand-written and some were typed. One letter was half typed and half written but all gave Helen descriptions of Grandpa's travels across the country. The postcards were in color and well preserved. Doug was mesmerized by the find. The one cent stamp on a postcard to Helen was upside down. This was an old fashion way of sending a letter with love.

Doug's curiosity was overflowing. He had found a wealth of information about this adventure and wondered if there were any additional stories about this trip on the Internet. Over the next few days, Doug sat down at a computer, opened a Google search window to search the Internet to see what he could find. He searched on the key words, "tuthill, maxwell, scull" and almost fell off his chair when the results showed the Ertl Toy Company was reproducing his Grandpa's Maxwell with all its signage as a toy bank. The car was #14 in the Texaco Collectors' Series that came with this description:

Texaco's relationship with motorsports began more than 75 years ago with this 1917 Maxwell Touring Car, fueled with and protected by Texaco products, P.G. Scull and C.W. Tuthill raced this vehicle from Newark, NJ, to Los Angeles, CA, setting a national record, the team completed its transcontinental journey in only 10 days and 16 hours. Texaco continues to offer both quality and dependability in the many products available to our loyal customers. This 14th in a series of quality antique bank vehicles is being offered exclusively by Texaco and should prove to be a very valuable addition to your collection. As one of our valued customers, we at Texaco thank you for choosing Texaco and look forward to being of service to you for many years to come.

Doug was amazed and at the same time chuckled to himself. For years, he went to countless car shows, and swap meets that often had a vendor pedaling toy cars. He imagined that it was very likely he walked right by this Maxwell toy bank never realizing it was a tribute to his Grandpa's adventure.

Trying different search words and following links in the search results revealed more stories about the trip as reported by newspapers across the country. "MAXWELL MOTOR CAR BUCKS WAY THROUGH 1000 MILES OF MUD" by the San Bernardino County Sun, "FAST TRIP ACROSS CONTINENT" by the San Francisco Chronicle, "THE OLD RELIABLE PULLED US THROUGH" by the Arizona Daily Star, "MAXWELL MAKES A NEW RECORD" by the Shreveport Times, "TRANSCONTINENTAL MAXWELL HERE", reported the Baltimore Sun and "FIRESTONE TIRES IN A GREAT TEST" by the Scranton Republican. There was a wealth of information about this trip in news print, but the most valuable find was Grandpa's hand written journal with the day by day account of the adventure.

Over the next few months, the discovery of all this history occupied Doug's thoughts. Being an antique car enthusiast it was natural to wonder whatever became of the Maxwell. What was it like to travel across the country prior to any interstate system of roads? How much fun it would be fun to experience such an adventure? Why not do this same trip again, in a Maxwell, on the 100th anniversary in 2016? This was the birth of Doug's dream adventure.

If Doug were to fulfill this dream, he needed a 1917 Maxwell Model 25 that could be made road worthy for the transcontinental trip. He wanted a 1917 Maxwell because he learned that Grandpa actually purchased a new 1917 year model in November of 1916. Doug used the power of the Internet to start his search. He found a listing for a 1917 Maxwell for sale at "Smiling Papa Johnson Ranch" in Elkhart, Kansas. Sadly, Papa Johnson told Doug, it had just been sold.

Through the Internet, Doug had the good fortune of finding Vern Campbell, who kept an updated Maxwell registry of all known Maxwells. This registry was a gold mine of owner names, addresses, some phone numbers, and Maxwell serial numbers! Doug thought maybe someone would be willing to sell theirs, and maybe even one of them could be identified as Grandpa's car.

Doug combed through the list of 1917 Maxwell Touring cars wondering if any of these cars could possibly be the car used by Grandpa. The next step was reaching out to the owners by mail to see if they were interested in selling their 1917 Maxwell. Each car was given a unique serial number that could be found on the bottom right side of the front seat near the floor board. Unfortunately with all the documentation found on Grandpa's trip so far, the serial number of the Maxwell used was not mentioned. Without this information, finding the actual car used for the trip was not very likely. On the other hand, Doug had a list of owners who might be willing to part with their Maxwell. Doug decided to send out a letter that explained he was looking for a 1917 Maxwell. The hope was to find a Maxwell that could be restored to a condition suitable to recreate the transcontinental trip in 2016. The letter asked if they would be willing to sell their Maxwell. Using the addresses in this registry of cars Doug sent out 10 letters to owners across the United States.

Continuing the search on the Internet, Doug located a second Maxwell in a museum; it was in the "Museum of Automobiles" in Morrilton, Arkansas. The

Maxwell was fully restored and in running condition. Doug and his mother, June, flew to Arkansas and Rich drove up from Austin Texas to meet the owner and look the car over.

1917 Maxwell in Arkansas

The Maxwell was in great shape and running. It was taken out and driven around the grounds. It was Doug's first experience with the feel of the car Grandpa drove.

Ideally Doug was looking for a Maxwell that was not fully restored, but was close to being road worthy. His car knowledge and skills meant he would consider a car that needed some work. Besides, he wanted the car to look like the original car used by Grandpa. This meant he would have to get this blue Maxwell repainted back to the basic black. The only color offered by Maxwell Motor Corporation in 1916. This would add to the cost of this Maxwell. By the end of the visit the decision was that this Maxwell was out of his target price range and he would have to keep looking.[1]

---

[1] As of 2016 this blue Maxwell can still be seen at the Museum of Automobiles in Morrilton, Arkansas

The first positive response to Doug's letters came not long after returning from Arkansas. It was from an owner in Lake Mills, Wisconsin by the name of Dale Anhalt. This was also a running Maxwell owned by a private individual, not a museum. Like the Maxwell in Arkansas this Maxwell was not the original black, but was a frame off restoration. This means that the body had been taken completely off the frame so it could be carefully cleaned and restored.

Second possible Maxwell for sale

In April of 2008, Doug took a trip to Wisconsin with Al Rodd to check out the car first hand. The car was in good shape. The canvas top was tan and showing signs of wear. It would pop out of second gear on occasion but was running and road worthy, at least for local car shows. The owner was fascinated with Doug's plans to take the car across country. When the owner's offer included a trailer a deal was struck. The Maxwell was loaded up for its journey to its new home on Long Island.

For the rest of 2008, the Maxwell was kept in the garage with an occasional outing like a winter ride with the family to pick out a Christmas tree. The transcontinental trip was still 7 years away and there was no real urgency to do any preparation. There would be time to do that so the Maxwell enjoyed a leisure life of an antique car that went to an occasional car show.

Maxwell sits and waits for preparation

Although Doug was not working actively on the Maxwell, he was frequently doing searches on the Internet for items he wanted to add to the car to make it look more like Grandpa's, based on the pictures in the photo album. Grandpa had a tool box on the passenger side running board that Doug desperately wanted to add to this car. A Klaxon Horn was another addition Grandpa installed on the driver's side running board. The horn was another "must have" to make the car look more like Grandpa's Maxwell. Then there was the radiator cap, a windshield spot light as well as different headlight lens. Unlike the Model T and Model A cars, finding Maxwell parts was not that easy. Doug kept vigil and frequently watched eBay, Craigslist, and car forums for old Maxwell parts. Doug frequently attended shows like the Antique Automobile Club of America meet in Hersey, Pennsylvania where there were literally hundreds of vendors pitching their automobile parts.

Doug's searches did meet with success over the years. In 2009 on eBay, he saw a Maxwell engine and transmission that were being auctioned. The engine and transmission were on a rolling stand and located in Indiana. Doug's bid won the auction. Doug picked up what he believed would be a backup engine for the transcontinental trip.

17

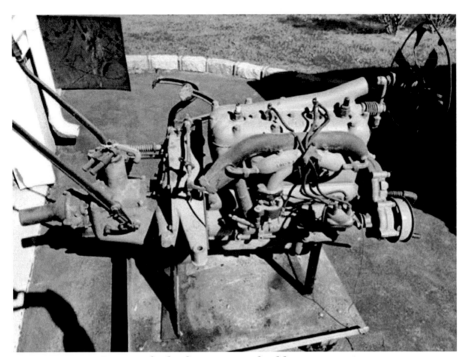

Despite the looks, a very valuable spare engine

Little did Doug know but the purchase of that spare engine turned out to be the best investment for this trip. As the story unfolds, that engine and transmission provided insights and parts both before and during the trip. Without that engine, the adventure would have been short lived.

In January, 2010, Doug published an article in the Old Cars Weekly. The article shared his desire to re-create his grandfather's trip. In the article, Doug asked for anyone with information about the original Maxwell or knowledge of the trip to contact him. Doug did not get any response. However, what Doug did not know was that another car enthusiast, by the name of Doug Johnson, in Indianapolis found the article interesting, and put a copy of it in his desk draw where it would sit for over six years.

The years melted away and little was done with the Maxwell. Doug would drive it once in a while but not much was done to prepare it for a transcontinental trip. Doug continued to watch his Internet sources for Maxwell parts. Doug found an authentic 1916 Klaxon horn and a tool box that was very close to being identical to Grandpa's tool box. With 2016 still years away there was not a lot of urgency to prepare for the journey.

It was not until the summer of 2015, a year and a half from the planned start that anything significant was done to the Maxwell. Although the Maxwell was running, Doug wanted to have the engine torn down, inspected, and rebuilt. A good friend and engine builder in Pennsylvania, Tony Bogovich from TNT Engineering made Doug a generous proposal. He offered to rebuild the Maxwell motor as his contribution to this adventure, as long as he could come along. That was an easy decision to make and in the summer of 2015, the engine was pulled and taken to Tony's shop in Pennsylvania. The Maxwell now sat lifeless in the garage with a gaping hole where the engine once sat, torn and tattered top, dry rotted tires and in need of a black paint job.

Chapter 3 – The Preparation

In January 2016 Doug's brother, Rich was starting his retirement after 38 years in the computer industry with a trip to Long Island from his home in Austin, Texas. Both boys had the same love of cars, car repairs, and restoration. Rich owned and maintained a 1955 Buick Special that was originally purchased by Grandpa Tuthill. The Buick was Rich's every day driver while attending school at Virginia Tech but he stored it in a barn behind his childhood house on Long Island after graduating and taking a job with IBM. It was not until years later, when Rich bought a house did the Buick come out of moth balls and was put in the house garage. As time allowed, Rich stripped the Buick in preparation for a new paint job. With a family of five, time to work on the Buick was limited. Eventually, it was painted a baby blue which accented the Dover White hard top. The Buick was the sixth member of the family and when Rich relocated the family to Austin, Texas, the Buick went along. Once in Austin, Rich found the time to put the Buick back on the road and drove it regularly throughout the year.

It was on that trip to New York that Doug and Rich discussed Doug's dream and all the work that was still pending. Doug realized that there were only eleven months to go if he was to leave on November 16th, the exact same day Grandpa and Scull started. He had no sponsors yet but believed Texaco would jump at the opportunity to celebrate the 100th anniversary of the same trip they endorsed in 1916. The Maxwell engine was still with Tony; a paint job was still needed, the top needed to be replaced; the drive train needed inspection; the tires needed replacement; the brakes, wheel bearing, and suspension all needed a close inspection. The punch list was long. With new-found time on his hands, Rich jumped in to help Doug live this dream. The two brothers started a collaboration that would have made Grandpa proud.

Up until 2016, the idea of getting a sponsor like Texaco and Firestone to help finance this adventure was on the "to-do" list but not aggressively pursued. Both boys believed that Texaco and Firestone would be eager to sponsor this trip because in 1992 Texaco was still showing actual pictures of C.W. Tuthill and P.G. Scull in their marketing material, citing how they have had 75 years of automobile racing heritage. Surely on the 100th year anniversary they could do still more marketing based on this recreation of history. However, before Doug and Rich could approach these big-name outfits they needed to put together a story, one might call a sales pitch. They needed to show prospective sponsors Grandpa's historic trip and the plans to recreate that epic adventure. They needed Internet exposure; they needed a website.

Rich used his experience with website development and started to build a web presence. While still visiting in New York Rich started to build out the website. It started with a full transcription of Grandpa's diary entries in two parts. Part one was the trip from Newark to Los Angeles, and part two was the return trip through the southern states. The boy's mother, June Tuthill Bassemir, was thrilled to see the interest her boys had taken to her father's trip. June shared stories of her dad and was a wealth of information and support. Like her boys, she enjoyed vintage cars and demonstrated her own skills with the restoration of a 1931 Model A Sports Coupe years ago. She enjoyed fixing things opposed to throwing them out. She had a knack for spotting treasures on those neighborhood trash days and frequently would bring home other people's junk and turn into a treasure. She was particularly instrumental in deciphering Grandpa's hand-written diary entries into Word documents on the computer. This made it easy for Rich to add the diary entries on the website.

By February, the newly created website described the story of C.W. Tuthill and P.G. Scull through diary entries. Visitors could read these entries, view pictures that were nearly 100 years old and browse through scanned copies of letters he had written while traveling.

In the proceeding days the website content grew. Doug and Rich decided to use the website to communicate the work being done to re-create this moment in history on the 100th anniversary. The boys also recognized how they would not be able to do this alone. A section on the website was created to recognize those folks that were helping make Doug's dream come true. Tony, who was rebuilding the engine, was one of the first folks listed. The boys anticipated that visitors to the website would like to know the planned route. Using Grandpa's diary, Rich had a list of thirty six towns, and twelve states that Grandpa mentioned. This allowed Rich to create a proposed route that would follow Grandpa's path while avoiding the use of interstate highways as much as possible. Doug and Rich imagined there would be some interest by folks to follow the progress of this adventure. Rich created a section on the website called "The Maxwell Chronicles." This section was the place where the boys would document their progress towards the November 16th start. Once the trip started, the "Maxwell Chronicles" would be used to document the trip as it progressed. By the end of February, there was enough content gathered to start directing folks to the website.

Rich started spreading the word. The goal was to build a network of car enthusiasts with technical experience and possibly tools or resources the boys would contact should they need help while en route. It was also hoped that they would generate enough interest so a potential sponsor could see the marketing opportunity.

By the beginning of March, just eight months prior to departure Rich started reaching out to the Chamber of Commerce for each town mentioned in Grandpa's diary. Rich created a spreadsheet from the list of thirty six towns. Using Google it was not difficult to find the different contact points for the town's Chamber of Commerce. Many would have a "Contact Us" link and Rich would write a message that typically looked like this one to the folks in Columbus, Ohio.

> *In 1916, my grandfather traveled from Newark, NJ to California in a 1917 Maxwell. Later this year, on the 100 year anniversary, we plan to make the same trip again in a restored 1917 Maxwell.*
>
> *One of the towns my grandfather mentions in his diary is Columbus, Ohio. We are anxious to visit as many landmarks as possible and could use some information about Columbus 100 years ago. Is there anyone who might be able to help us understand Columbus 100 years ago? For example, what were the major roads in and out of town back then? Are there any 100-year-old historic landmarks that we might visit?*
>
> *We are open to any information you can share or questions you might have about this trip.*
>
> *Thank you for your time and consideration.*

By mid March, Rich had emailed twenty seven towns on his spreadsheet. The response to Rich's request for information was very positive and encouraging. Many of the emails applauded the idea and thought it was a great tribute to the boy's grandfather. Rich did not see a response from every town but the ones that responded were insightful. Often the responses included contact information for local historical societies, museums, associations and car clubs.

Many of these towns responded, not only with encouraging replies but also with helpful names of people and organizations. The folks in Pittsburgh were having a bicentennial celebration and invited Rich to put the Maxwell in their bicentennial parade in July. Rich was also put in contact with the Lincoln Highway Association since the Lincoln Highway was the route Grandpa took through Pennsylvania. Rich's spreadsheet had names, email addresses, and phone numbers of folks across the country: The Pittsburgh History and Landmarks Foundation, Ohio Historical Society, Indianapolis Chamber of Commerce, Missouri Historical Society, Lyon County Historical Museum (near Emporia, Kansas) and San Bernardino Historical and Pioneer Society to name a few. Some towns sent local literature to Rich via the post office. Local car clubs were also contacted. Through March and April Rich spent hours sending emails, responding to emails and talking directly to folks all along the route gathering valuable information that was used to plan this trip. Rich's spreadsheet of contacts grew from thirty six to well over hundred.

The New Jersey Historical Society which was located in Newark, New Jersey was of particular interest and one of the first contacted by Doug. Doug reached out to them to help identify where the Maxwell Dealership was located as well as any insights they might have had about Newark in 1916. The boys would learn later that the New Jersey Historical Society building was just a block from where C.W. Tuthill and P.G. Scull started their transcontinental trip, 544 Broad Street, which back in 1916 was the location of the Maxwell Dealership where Tuthill and Scull worked.

Over the next few weeks Rich would gather valuable information from the growing list of supporters. Jeanne Finstein from the Friends of Wheeling was very helpful in identifying the route Grandpa had to have taken to cross the Ohio River into Wheeling, West Virginia one hundred years ago. The only way to cross the Ohio River would have been across the 1849 Suspension Bridge which was still in use. Jeanne checked around for local antique car clubs to possibly arrange for an old car parade across the bridge depending on our schedule. Rich started a list of photo opportunities. The suspension bridge was the first on the list.

Mark Dollase from the Indianapolis Landmarks organization responded to Rich's request for the location of the Oneida Hotel that was mentioned by Grandpa in his diary. Unfortunately, the hotel was no longer standing in downtown Indianapolis. It was replaced by the Pan Am Plaza on the

Southwest corner of West Georgia Street and South Illinois Street. Mark also provided information and contacts for the Indiana National Road Association and the Indiana Automotive organizations for more background about the area and possible meet and greets. Rich's spreadsheet of contacts continued to grow.

Gloria Forouzan from the City of Pittsburgh was delighted with the boy's plans and asked if it would be possible to bring the Maxwell to Pittsburgh on July 9th to be part of the city's Bicentennial Parade and the centennial celebration of the City Hall which would have been under construction when Grandpa passed by. Rich was excited about the offer, but it was doubtful they would be ready and have the time to participate.

Emily Jaycox at the Missouri Historical Society was particularly resourceful and did research that helped clarify entries in Grandpa's diary. According to what Emily found the only bridge into St. Louis in 1916 was the Eads Bridge. Rich noted that and updated their route, so they were sure to take that bridge across the Mississippi River. Grandpa mentioned in his diary how they ate lunch at "Thompsons". At first Rich thought that was a town, but Emily found that in 1916 there was a restaurant called Thompsons Dairy and Luncheonette that was on Washington Avenue just a few blocks after crossing the Eads Bridge. Rich's hopes of eating there were dashed when Emily explained that section of downtown was rebuilt into the America's Center Convention Complex. Emily also identified the most probable route through town Grandpa would have made in 1916. It was Route 180. Rich made note of the road on their route plans. Emily also sent Rich copies of St. Louis maps from 1916.

The Lyon County Historical Society responded with pictures of Emporia Kansas in the 1900's as well as suggestions on the roads to take through Kansas.

One of Grandpa's pictures showed him in Lamar, Colorado standing in front of his Maxwell with the Savoy Hotel in the background. Sarah Gilmor, a reference librarian at the History of Colorado responded to Rich's request for the location of the Savoy Hotel in Lamar. Sarah found the street address from a 1918 business directory. Rich looked up that address on Google Maps and looked at the street view. The street looked nothing like the picture of the Savoy Hotel in Grandpa's photo. Instead of a three-story building there was a two-story motel called the "Buzzard's Nest" offering weekly and monthly rates, with cable TV and wifi. Rich guessed over the past 100 years the block was totally rebuilt. It was not until months later Rich would find out from other Lamar residents that he was actually looking at the wrong location.

As the days progressed, Rich continued to circulate the story by sharing the website address with the Discovery Channel, Vintage Race Car Magazine, Coker Tire, Lincoln Highway Heritage Center, the History Channel and Trip Advisor. The hope was that one of these outfits would pick up on the story and sponsor the adventure in one way or another. Although responses were encouraging most added that they do not take unsolicited submissions. That did not discourage Rich, who continued to circulate the story, anyway.

Rich searched the Antique Automobile Club of America (AACA) and learned there was a local chapter in Austin, Texas. The president was Joe Peter, and the Central Texas chapter name was called the Road Relics. Rich emailed Joe, which resulted in a delightful phone conversation. Joe invited Rich to attend their April meeting.

Having never undertaken a cross-country trip in an antique car, Doug and Rich were anxious to learn from other antique car owners' experience. What went right, what problems they had, anything that would help the boys prepare for the trip. Joe Peter from the AACA was instrumental in introducing Rich to Ray Terry at Dick's Classic Garage Car Museum, a fantastic museum in San Marcos, Texas. The museum founder and president is Dick Burdick, who, with Ray participated in multiple Great Races. Their experiences driving antique cars across the country meant they would be a great source of advice and suggestions for Doug and Rich as they prepared the Maxwell for this trip. Rich made arrangements to meet with Ray face-to-face in the museum when Doug planned to come to Austin in April.

Although the website was in place it was undergoing daily updates as the plans were evolving. New supporters and notes were added to the planned route, and pictures were posted. Doug's planned visit to Austin in April included participation in the annual Lonestar Roundup Car Show. The boys planned on driving Grandpa's 1955 Buick as it was a great opportunity to talk about the pending adventure. To help spread the word, Rich ordered business cards with the website address so the boys could distribute these during the car show.

March ended with an intriguing email from John Harper, Historian for the Chevron Corporation which owned the Texaco brand. John had heard about our plans and wanted to talk. The circulation of the boys' plans looked like it hit pay dirt, with a direct line into Chevron and the Texaco brand. This was exciting news. With John's support, getting a sponsorship looked good. Doug was booked on a flight to Austin in a week so Rich responded to John asking to set up the call at his convenience when Doug was in Austin. John said he would arrange a time to call and talk over the phone. When Doug arrived in Austin, they reached out to John about the call time. Unfortunately the boys never heard back from him.

April started with an email from Nick Cataldo a San Bernardino resident with vast knowledge of the National Old Trails Road and Cajon Pass, which was the route Grandpa had taken. Nick had written about the National Old Trails Road and the history of the San Bernardino area. This was the start of a new friendship with Nick providing valuable insights for the boy's plans. He later offered suggestions while they were en route.

A car club in Emporia, Kansas called the Emporia Flatland Cruisers had heard about the trip and sent an email to Rich offering assistance in any way on the trip. It was exactly the kind of response Doug and Rich were hoping to get. Rich added their contact information to the route itinerary should they need help when in or around Emporia.

Doug arrived in Austin in early April. The day after he arrived, he and Rich attended the annual Lonestar Round Up. It is a huge three day outdoor car show and festival featuring vintage hot rods and custom cars pre 1963. The boys drove Grandpa's 1955 Buick Special each day, found a place to park on the grassy field and spent hours walking around looking at over 1200 vintage and custom cars. The boys kept their eye out for Maxwell parts they may have wanted as "spares", interacted with fellow car enthusiasts and passed out business cards. They were not surprised to find one vendor who was selling toy automobiles. Among the cars on his table was Grandpa's Maxwell.

Doug sits Doug in Grandpa's 1955 Buick

While Doug was visiting Central Texas, the boys made a point to travel to San Marcos to meet the chief mechanic at Dick's Classic Automobile Car Museum. Ray Terry not only maintains the classic cars in the museum, but he also teamed with the founder Dick Burdick in multiple Great Races. Ray was very familiar with driving cross-country. He was also a very valuable source of information. The most common failure he experienced was overheating cars.

Doug and Ray from Dick's Garage

Doug and Rich bombarded Ray with questions. What kinds of failures might be expected? Should a 12 volt system be installed? (the Maxwell ran on 6 volts) Not only was Ray gracious, but he walked the boys through the shop and pointed out changes he implemented in the cars used for the Great Race. His coffee was pretty good too. After a couple of hours with Ray, Doug and Rich left with multiple ideas to consider implementing on the Maxwell. For example installing an electric water pump and installing an alternator to run a 12 volt system. The boys "to do" list was growing but the engine was still with Tony. They would have to wait to implement these suggestions.

While the boys did not hear back from John Harper at Chevron during the time Doug was in Austin, they did connect up with a terrific gentleman in San Bernardino, Allen Born. The San Bernardino Chamber of Commerce had forwarded the request for information back in March to Allen. The two boys called Allen and talked at length about the trip and their plans. Allen graciously spent time with Rich, Doug, and Google maps to show the boys a suggested route from Victorville, California through the Cajon Pass to San Bernardino via Route 66. Allen extended an offer for lunch if they would stop at the San Bernardino Rail Station where they have a History and Railroad Museum. Rich added this to their route plans.

Doug and Rich realized they needed to think about the cost of this adventure. They worked on a budget. After all, they needed to be prepared for a sponsor's questions about expenses for the trip. The starting plan would be to drive the Maxwell, a chase truck with trailer, and a motor home. They estimated a ten-day trip out with all three vehicles and returning with the Maxwell on the trailer in four days. Considering the mileage they might expect for each vehicle and gas prices, then adding in hotel rooms and meals the dollar signs started to add up. They wanted two men for each vehicle so there could be some driver rotation. The figure they arrived at was $14,000 but there were a lot of variables. How often might they stay in the motor home? Would they need one or two hotel rooms? Price of gas, how much should they allow for meals, and what about oil, and grease? Lining up four other guys willing to make the trip did not appear to be a problem as many had expressed an interest in joining. The motor home needed some repairs to be road worthy. Jeff Grathwohl at Jamesport Auto was a valuable resource in helping prepare a motor home.

After Doug returned to Long Island, Rich attended his first AACA meeting of the Road Relics. They were welcoming and a source of advice and suggestions for the trip. Rich joined the Road Relics chapter that evening and later learned that Doug was already a member of the Peconic AACA chapter on Long Island.

As April progressed, Rich continued to reach out to many towns' Chamber of Commerce. Rich also started to post messages on popular antique car forums such as the HAMB forum at the Jalopy Journal and the Antique Automobile Club of America (AACA). To leverage the power of social media, Rich started to use Facebook and Twitter feeds on Texaco and Firestone to generate interest and support for this adventure.

The efforts were generating comments and words of encouragement on the website. One very interesting comment came from Bob Larimore in Springfield, Ohio. Unknown to the boys, Bob Larimore was also intrigued by the C.W. Tuthill and P.G. Scull story before the website was ever started. Bob had a Maxwell himself and was in the process of painting the Maxwell to look like the Maxwell used in 1916. Bob expressed a concern that the boys would not like the idea but to the contrary, Doug and Rich were thrilled that there was a second effort under way to credit the incredible adventure of their grandfather in 1916. There was an immediate connection between them as they shared stories and technical information about their respective projects. Bob's knowledge of the Maxwell was welcomed, and he also offered some of his spare Maxwell parts. What was even more amazing was that Bob was located in Springfield, which was one of the towns Grandpa had passed through in 1916. Rich made another note to their route plans to stop in to see Bob. This would be another photo opportunity with not one but two look alike Maxwells.

The spare motor Doug had bought shortly after buying the Maxwell was still tucked away in the corner of the garage. With the original motor still with Tony, Doug thought that motor should be considered as a backup if by chance there was an issue with the motor Tony was rebuilding. Doug pulled off the inspection plate on the transmission and found a name inscribed on the back. Howard E. Darby in Norwood, Ohio engraved his name and date, April 16th, 1921. A search on the Internet reveled that Howard worked at the Cincinnati Bickford Tool Company and had a patent on a shifter mechanism. This could very well have been a transmission Howard worked on while developing that patent.

Doug loaded the engine and transmission on a truck and took it over to T-Jays Transmissions in Riverhead. Doug had done business with Jay Tranchina in the past, and Jay was willing to look over the transmission and let Doug know what kind of shape it was in. The engine's fan was pretty mangled, and the engine crank shaft would turn but Doug had no idea what it would take to get it running. For now, he needed Jay to look at the clutch and transmission. It might make a suitable spare if the transmission Tony had with the engine he was working on should have a problem. Little did Doug know this engine, as bad as it might look, was a life saver a couple of times over.

John Raffel, who used to work with Rich at IBM back in the 70s, learned about this trip. John now lived in the Kansas City area with valuable knowledge of Kansas City, as well as great places to eat. Being a local resident of the area, John knew the scenic back roads that would avoid an attempt to drive through Kansas City using interstate highways. John suggested a much more scenic route on the Blue River Parkway. He and Rich exchanged emails and phone conversations that allowed Rich to update the route on the website.

Doug and Rich were aware of the fact that Texaco might not come through with financial support. Although there was still hope John Harper would respond, the boys needed to explore other ways to raise funds for the trip. Doug worked with a local printer to investigate the creation of a graphic to be put on a shirt that would have Grandpa's picture and the caption "making history again." Doug connected up with a local outfit and ordered custom Red Kapp work shirts with a picture of Grandpa in the Maxwell. By selling these shirts, money could be generated. Every little bit would help.

Rich monitored the number of users going to the website to see what kind of interest was being produced by this adventure. Rich was excited to see in April that 529 users visited the site and viewed almost 1,800 pages. This spike was largely driven by a posting made in a Hemmings Blog by Daniel Strohl on April 16th about the transcontinental road trip story. Rich reviewed daily messages sent in from readers of the website with well wishes and offers for help while en route. Joe Hudson was one such reader who was looking forward to following the adventure along with his Thanksgiving dinner. Even though he was in Cincinnati, he offered help if needed while the boys passed through Ohio. Suggestions came from all directions on what to wear, what roads to take, mechanical changes to implement on the Maxwell, even offers for food. Rich updated the website to allow interested readers to subscribe. By subscribing they would automatically be sent an email with updates once the trip started. By the end of April there were 29 subscribers. The website had not gone viral but the boys were delighted to see others were interested in following the adventure.

In the month of May, the Maxwell started its transformation. First order of business was to remove the canopy, doors and dash so the parts could be wet sanded in preparation for a black paint job. As the Maxwell was being prepared for its black paint job, Rich continued to spread the word of the website with more Facebook, Twitter, and blog posts. Juan Barraza, the editor of the Road Relics newsletter (the Central Texas Antique Automobile Club of America chapter) published a short article that Rich wrote about the trip with a link to the website in the May newsletter.

C.W. Tuthill and P.G. Scull were not the first to cross the country in an automobile. There were others with their own purpose and challenges. One particular transcontinental trip intrigued Rich. In 2009, Emily Anderson drove a 1909 Maxwell from New York City to San Francisco celebrating the 100th year anniversary of the same trip done by Alice Ramsey in 1909. Alice was the first woman to travel across the country in an automobile. Emily's father, Richard Anderson was the one to essentially rebuild the 1909 Maxwell Model DA which was no easy task. The similarities of the two adventures interested Rich. Both trips celebrated a 100th year anniversary. Rich found an article about Emily's trip written by Terry Parkhurst and emailed Terry to tell him about the plans to do another 100th year anniversary run to celebrate Grandpa's accomplishment, and Terry and Rich eventually connected up with a phone call. It was an insightful phone call for Rich to hear Terry's perspective on Emily's trip, but even more valuable was that Terry gave Rich a contact for Emily's dad, which led to a phone call with Richard Anderson.

Richard Anderson enthusiastically accepted the opportunity to talk with Rich. For almost an hour, Rich listened about the 2009 adventure eager to learn from their experience. It was an insightful call. For example, the boys wondered how many tires they should plan on taking. Richard said that Emily did the entire trip on a single set of tires. Rich asked, "If you were to do it again, what would you do differently?" Richard Anderson's reply surprised Rich. "Emily and I asked ourselves that same question," said Mr. Anderson, "If we were to do it again," Mr. Anderson replied, "Both Emily and I agreed that it should be done privately."

Apparently with all the publicity and interest generated, deadlines, appointments, and schedules added stress to the trip. This caused Rich to reflect on all his efforts to share the plans for this recreation of history. From that day on, Doug and Rich were careful about making specific commitments to folks that wanted to meet and greet us along the way. The boys very much wanted to hook up with folks, especially those that were helping, but they also wanted to stay true to the goal of completing the trip in 10 days. The reality was that they might not have time to socialize.

As the month of May came to a close, Rich watched the traffic to the website as an indicator on how well the word was spreading. Clearly, the website had not gone viral, but during the month of May, there were over 175 visitors and a dozen comments with words of encouragement. By the end of May, subscriptions rose to 31.

The beginning of June was an exciting time for the Maxwell. The cream colored car got the last of its wet sanding. Doug transported the body, doors, hood, and black paint to Chris Urban. Chris had offered to paint the Maxwell as his contribution to the adventure. When Chris finished, the Maxwell glistened like it would have in 1916.

The Maxwell goes back to black

Rich flew up to Long Island in June and spent time with Doug going over the new black beauty. The boys put the rear fenders back on, and installed the gas tank, the windshield, and the steering column. The wheels were removed so the wheel bearings could be inspected and re-packed with fresh grease. The doors remained off because the Texaco and Firestone lettering needed to be painted. It would be easier to have the signage put on the doors while they were not on the Maxwell. Doug was still looking for an artist to do that work.

Maxwell coming back together

Now the Maxwell was in need of a new set of tires. The existing ones had plenty of tread but featured old and dry rotted sidewalls. These might have been on the wheels for 50 or more years! Using such tires to drive across the country was not a good idea. New tires were going to be a significant expense, so the boys hoped that Firestone would donate a set. Rich thought about using social media to reach out to Firestone. The Firestone brand was owned by Bridgestone. Rich posted a comment on their Facebook page telling the story and providing a link to the website. Bridgestone responded to the boys' plea for a sponsorship with a polite rejection. They said they were committed to supporting initiatives in education, youth development, and environment and conservation. The boys faced the reality they did not have the same salesman skills their Grandpa possessed. They wondered if pushing the Maxwell across the USA would have changed their decision. With no support from the Firestone brand, the boys needed to look for another source. Rich reached out to Coker Tire in hopes it would be interested in this trip and would donate tires and tubes, a significant expense. Rich posted a request for sponsorship on the Coker Tire Facebook page and waited with baited breath for a response.

With still no sponsorship the boys thought they would test the water and look for a sponsor other than Texaco. The problem was that they wanted the Maxwell to look like the original which had Firestone and Texaco logos on the doors. This could be a problem with a different sponsor. Regardless, Rich reached out to O'Reilly's Auto Parts. O'Reilly's told Rich that money allocated for these kinds of events was at the local region. They prefer to sponsor activity at the local level. This was an unfortunate response and might have been different if they only knew how O'Reilly's came to the rescue during the trip.

Still looking for ways to share the story and gather support, Rich thought about writing up an article for The Antique Automobile Club of America online newsletter called "The Speedster." Before the month of June closed, Rich submitted a story about the planned trip. The Speedster editor, Stacy Zimmerman, was excited about the article and told Rich it would be published in an upcoming issue. Stacy asked for a follow-up article after the adventure was over.

As June came to a close, the traffic on the website settled in with 105 visitors. The number of subscribers to the website climbed to 32. It was nothing viral, but the grandsons found it encouraging that a growing number of people were interested in the adventure and wanted to follow along with the planned blogs.

July arrived with the realization that there were less than six months to prepare for a departure on November 16th. The boys created a punch list of things still to accomplish. It seemed like more items were added to the list than they were able to scratch off.

The exciting news in July came from Coker Tire. Coker had the original 30x3 1/2 Firestone tires, and although they did not wish to be a full sponsor, they did offer the boys a nice discount price on a set of five tires, tubes and a tire warranty. Based on Richard Anderson's experience in 2009, and because the roads the boys would be using were in better shape, five tires would be plenty. The tire warranty was a safety net. Little did they know it would turn out to be a blessing to have that warranty on the first day of the trip. Before the end of July, five gorgeous Firestone tires and tubes arrived.

Doug located a metal tool box with old style clasps to hold the lid closed on eBay. It was black and looked nearly identical to the toolbox on Grandpa's Maxwell. June used her artistic talents and copied the lettering on the original tool box to paint "Economy Auto Supply" with the address on the box. The tool box looked identical to the original 1916 version. Doug had earlier tried to find the "Economy Auto Supply" business but was unsuccessful even though Grandpa's pictures showed an address for the store. Maybe it was bought up by a big chain auto parts store.

June's skillful lettering of the tool box

More great news in July came when Doug was able to find a local artist that would paint the doors, hood, and Maxwell cowl just as it was in 1916. His name was Jim Fetten, and his skill was at painting incredible fire truck graphics and lettering. Doug could not have found a better person for the job. Doug left the doors and hood with Jim in July with plans for Jim to come to the house to do the lettering on the Maxwell cowl.

Back in Austin, Rich received an email from Dan Kruse Classics auction house looking for antique cars to sell in an auction in September. Rich had the 1955 Buick Special that Grandpa had bought new. It sat in a barn for years before Rich took ownership of the car from his grandmother in 1973. The Buick was rust free and in running condition with only 60,000 miles on it. For the last 43 years, Rich had cared for the car and kept it running. With still no sponsor Rich thought it might be the time to sell the Buick and use those funds to cover some of the costs of this adventure. The Buick was worth more sentimentally to Rich than anyone would ever pay, and he did not ever think he would sell it. It was a standing joke that he was to be buried in the Buick. On the other hand, the idea of selling a car that Grandpa had purchased to fund a recreation of one of Grandpa's accomplishments made the idea of selling the Buick more bearable. Rich registered the Buick for the auction before the end of the month.

Grandpa's Buick ready for the auction

July was a slow month for any website promotional activity by Rich. Getting a connection with Coker Tire was the only significant activity. The website traffic in July reflected that, with just 107 visitors to the website and only three new subscribers, which raised the total number of subscribers to 35.

If there was one word to describe the month of August, it would be "presentations". With less than four months to launch and still no sponsors Rich and Doug took to presenting their plans in hopes of generating interest in the trip and potentially a lead on a sponsor. Rich presented a program to the Central Austin Antique Automobile Club of America, the Road Relics. The group was supportive and encouraging. Towards the end of the month, Doug and Rich attended the Long Island Model A club monthly meeting and told the story of the transcontinental trip in 1916 and the plans to repeat history. The club was enthusiastic over the trip and purchased half a dozen shirts to help fund the adventure.

To increase visibility in the social media area, Rich created a public Facebook page for Grandpa. Grandpa, or "cwtutill" now had an identity in the 21st century. On this page, Rich planned to add pictures and videos to share the adventure with the Facebook community.

Emails to Chevron and to John Harper in corporate had gone unanswered. Apparently, what Rich and Doug thought would be a "no brainer" for Texaco had, for some reason, not sparked any interest. Rich decided to try the Texaco Facebook page to communicate plans in hopes the grandsons could get a decision from Texaco on a possible sponsorship. Reaching out via a Facebook message to Texaco finally resulted with a reply. The reply was a generic, "not interested" response. This was the response that the boys feared the most. It just seemed to them that Texaco was missing out on a marketing opportunity that equaled similar opportunities leveraged in the past. As disappointing as that response was, it did not deter Rich and Doug from moving forward. On the bright side, they pictured photo opportunities on the coming trip at Mobil and Exxon gas stations. In addition, without Texaco in the picture, they would have more freedom to what they wanted to do on the trip, and not be controlled by a sponsor's demands. This would be a good thing.

Joe Peter from the Road Relics emailed Rich with information about a casting call taking place in Austin. From what Joe had found out, a production company was looking for local stories of interest. Rich followed up on the casting call from Leftfield Pictures. They were shooting a show in Austin and were looking for a local Austin story for a TV series they were shooting. Rich talked with Molly Tom a Casting Associate Producer. It was a fun interview over the phone and Molly thought what the boys were doing was a great story. But would it fit the story they needed for their TV show? A few days later, the answer was that this story was not a good fit for this show, but they liked the story and said they might follow up with the boys later.

In August, the Maxwell took on its reincarnated identity when Jim finished the signage for the doors and hood. His work looked fantastic, and the Maxwell was looking more and more like Grandpa's Maxwell.

Doug's wife Maria displays the new signage

Rich flew out to Long Island at the end of August to spend more time on the Maxwell with Doug. The driver-side front leaf spring was weak and gave the Maxwell a bit of a lean so the boys removed the spring and took it to a shop in Riverhead to have it reshaped. The Maxwell was getting ready for its first public appearance the following weekend at a Boy Scout sponsored car show in Southold, Long Island. In anticipation of more opportunities to promote the adventure, another batch of business cards was ordered, this time with Doug's contact information.

By the time August came to a close the website traffic was showing signs that the presentations during the month were driving more interest. Visitors to the website were up to 187 and subscriptions had grown to 40. Perhaps not earth shattering but it was inspiring to see the interest grow.

The theme for September was "car shows". With the Maxwell painted, and the doors and hood on with fantastic signage, it was ready for a couple of car shows. Of course, Doug and Rich had to explain the missing engine and took a couple of friendly quips about their gas mileage. One fellow asked if they were going to push it across the country, but it was all in fun, and participants at the shows were genuinely interested in the boys' undertaking, and wished the boys luck on the trip.

The first show was run by the Boy Scouts in Southold at the Parks and Recreation Center. Doug had a banner made that summed up the adventure that was under way. The boys had to trailer the car to Southold and roll it off the trailer. June attended the show as the daughter of C.W. Tuthill, and she answered many questions as folks gathered around the car to hear the story of the cross-country trip in 1916. Business cards were passed out so the folks could visit the website and read C.W. Tuthill's diary and the plans to recreate the adventure in more detail.

Maxwell debuts at its first car show

Rich returned to Austin the following week in order to take the 1955 Buick to the Dan Kruse Classics auction. Watching the clean Buick roll up on the auction block gave Rich a lump in his throat. The Buick held many memories and to watch it get auctioned off was hard for Rich. The auctioneer started his routine and worked the bidders up to $7,250. The auctioneer looked at Rich, and he gave the no thanks nod. Rich had previously set the reserve at $11,000 based on earlier appraisals so the current bid was below expectations. They would run the Buick again later in the afternoon, and it might go for more.

Rich left the auction unwilling to watch the Buick roll back on the auction platform for the afternoon bidding. It was on the drive home when Rich got a call from the auction house saying they had a buyer, but his offer was lower at $6,250. Just like a car salesman, the auction house needed an immediate answer. Not willing to make an immediate decision he put them off so he could call Doug and get his opinion. The grandsons had no sponsorship, and the $6250 would help fund the adventure even though it was not as much as hoped. It was Grandpa's way of helping his grandsons with this adventure. Rich took the offer, and the following day said his good-byes to the Buick and signed off on the paperwork.

On the brighter side, a friend of Rich, Bryan Moore, heard about the Buick and expressed an interest in buying it. Within a week, this friend agreed on a price with the new owner and purchased the Buick. The Buick would stay in Austin with a new family that was excited to get the classic. Rich was thrilled the Buick was going to a family where it would hopefully generate as many memories as it did for Rich.

Back on Long Island, Doug attended the Peconic Bay AACA meeting and presented Grandpa's story and the plans to re-create history. The club was excited about the adventure offering advice and encouragement. The following weekend Doug took the Maxwell off to its second car show at the Hallockville Museum Farm on Long Island.

June with Gina, and Becca, two of Doug's children

The Maxwell drew a lot of attention with the occasional question, "Where's the engine?" One particular passerby was Joe Limongelli from the Automobile Hall of Fame. Joe, also known as GT Joey is known for driving a Ford GT around the world. Joe was excited to hear about this adventure and invited Doug to bring the Maxwell to yet another car show coming up in October. The car show was billed as "Back in Time, Before 49." Joe would be the host of the show. Even more exciting was that Joe gave Doug a lead to connect with Jay Leno once in Los Angeles. The thought of meeting Jay Leno at the conclusion of the cross-country trip would certainly be the icing on the cake.

After the Hallockville car show, Doug took the Maxwell over to T-Jay's Transmission. Jay had looked over the transmission on the spare engine Doug had dropped off earlier. Jay reported that the gears in the transmission were in very good shape with little wear. This was good news and got Doug to thinking that perhaps this transmission should be used with the engine Tony was working on. The purpose of taking the Maxwell over to Jay's was to get his opinion on the gears in the rear end. Multiple folks over the last few months that heard about the plans suggested that a weak point on the Maxwell was the ring and pinion gear in the rear end. More than one person suggested the boys ought to have spare gears. If they had a ring gear fail en route, the trip would be over. The hope was that Jay would find the current gears in good shape like the transmission gears on the spare engine.

Doug called on Tony to find out the status of the engine being rebuilt. Tony said it would be back together in another week or so. Shortly after that Tony called Doug to tell him the engine had a cracked head. This would have been a show stopper had Doug not had the spare engine. Doug went to Jay's shop, removed the head from the spare engine, and made an emergency trip to Pennsylvania to give Tony this second head. Thank goodness for the spare engine.

Towards the end of September, Rich flew back to Long Island to help Doug work on the punch list as well as participate in car shows coming up in October. The Maxwell still had the old tires that needed to be replaced with the new Coker tires. Replacing tires on the Maxwell was a task Grandpa did multiple times during his trip. Putting new tubes and tires on the rims was going to be a first for the boys. They prepared by watching how this was done by others on YouTube videos. It did not look too hard, as long as they had tire irons. Doug had purchased three earlier in the month. However, the videos did not show anyone taking an old tire off that had been on the rim for maybe fifty years. Doug and Rich started with the spare rim and managed to get the old tire off after thirty minutes of pounding, prying and pulling. The tire had been on the rim for so long it was as if the rubber melted into the metal rim. It took almost as much effort to get the new tube and tire installed on the rim. Success took just over an hour, and the boys wondered how Grandpa managed to do this eight times in one day as he mentioned in his diary. Although the boys felt a sense of satisfaction with getting the first tire done, what they failed to do was inspect the spare rim. If they had done that inspection, they would have seen the razor-sharp edge on the inner rim that ultimately would be the cause of their first breakdown on the trip.

The following day, the remaining tires were removed from the rims so the rims could be cleaned up and painted. Getting all the old tires off required a bit of sweat equity, but they were removed without having to resort to using a sawzall to cut them off, an option the boys seriously considered. Even with the practice of removing the remaining tires from the rims the boys agreed that Grandpa probably would have chuckled to see how they struggled to get them off.

It was the last day of September when Rich had a phone conversation with his cousin Bruce Tuthill, another C.W. Tuthill grandson. Bruce was the first grandson and was very supportive of this re-creation of history honoring their grandfather. It was on this call that Rich was encouraged to start a GoFundMe account. This is a social tool that would allow followers on the Internet to make a contribution to this adventure. Doug and Rich had considered this option earlier in the year but at that time neither grandson liked the idea of "begging" for support. However, on this call, Bruce, and his financial adviser Tony, got Rich to thinking that maybe this was not such a bad idea. Yes, the Buick had been sold but those funds would not cover all their costs. The Maxwell still needed a replacement top which the boys thought might cost $2,000. Rich opened an account with a goal of $5,000 to help pay for the gas, oil and supplies for the Maxwell. The response was terrific and within days, friends were making generous contributions.

When September came to a close the website recorded 106 users to the website and subscribers increased to 46 users who wanted to be kept up to date on the progress of this trip. The GoFundMe account had already received a few hundred dollars in donations.

October arrived, and work on the Maxwell went into high gear. Rich was still in town and helped Doug install the remaining new Firestone tires as well as mounting the Klaxon horn on the running board and hooking up the electrical connections in time for a third car show. This show was in Bridgehampton. It was called the annual Bridgehampton Road Rally. The weather prediction was not good with rain expected. Perhaps not the best day to trailer the Maxwell to a show but both Doug and Rich thought if the threat of rain was going to discourage them; they had no right to drive the Maxwell across the country in who knows what kind of weather. They took the Maxwell to the event. The threat of rain clearly reduced the number of spectators. Those who did attend talked up a storm and were encouraging about this trip. By 2 PM, the boys had the Maxwell back on the trailer heading home.

The Bridgehampton show was on Saturday. Sunday morning the Maxwell was back on the trailer heading to Cutchogue, Long Island for the "Back in Time, Before 49" car show hosted by GT Joey. The weather had cleared, and the turnout was significantly better for this show. More business cards were passed out and a couple of the fund raising shirts were sold.

Back in time car show

The first two days of October were occupied with car shows. On the third of October, Tony arrived with the long awaited, rebuilt engine. Although the engine was back there was still work to be done. The boys still needed to attach the clutch, transmission, carburetor, starter/generator, radiator and more. The transmission and clutch were separated, which gave the boys a chance to inspect those parts. The cone clutch appeared to be in very good shape with little wear. The transmission gears were another story. Even to the untrained eye one could see significant wear on the gears. Doug recalled how the Maxwell would sometimes pop out of second gear while driving it. Looking at the gears one would understand why that would happen. Second gear was badly worn. The next decision was easy. They would use the transmission from the spare engine that Jay said was in great shape. Thank goodness for that spare engine again.

The Maxwell was still in need of a new top. One of the local supporters, Erich Cramer, suggested taking the Maxwell to a place in Greenport that specializes in canvas tops for boats. Doug and Rich installed the existing top and loaded the Maxwell on the trailer to show Mills Canvas the top and discuss prices. After the 40-minute drive to Greenport and showing the folks the top, they decided it was not something they wanted to tackle and suggested the boys take it to Southampton Upholstery.

On the return trip from Greenport, Doug talked with Chris (who painted the Maxwell) on the phone. Chris suggested Doug talk to Rob Wood about making a new top for the Maxwell. It turns out the boys would be passing by Rob's place on the way back from Greenport. How convenient! They stopped to see Rob. After inspecting the top, Rob offered to do it for at a bargain price. All they would have to do is remove the old top from the frame, so he could use it as a pattern. Finding someone to make a new top was a major accomplishment. It was another item to cross off the punch list.

Another task on the punch list was to go through the entire Maxwell electrical system. Fortunately in Doug's ongoing quest for Maxwell parts he bought a Maxwell owner's manual. It included complete wiring diagrams.

One unique aspect of the Maxwell was the electrical system to crank the engine. To start the Maxwell engine the driver would have to depress a pedal on the floor to the right of the gas pedal with their foot. Pressing that pedal engaged the starter's gear with the fly wheel and at the same time supplied voltage to the starter motor to crank the engine. The Maxwell had a six volt electrical system to supply power to the lights and ignition, but needed twelve volts to energize the starter motor. The Maxwell accomplished this by using two six volt batteries and a mechanical switch that would connect those two six volt batteries in series when the driver depressed the starter pedal. This action provided twelve volts to energize the starter motor and crank the engine. When the engine started and the driver released the starter pedal, the starter switch puts those two six volt batteries in parallel to supply just six volts to the Maxwell for the lights and ignition. While going over the wiring Rich tested this starter switch and found that it was faulty. Rich opened up the starter switch and saw the copper contacts inside had broken and no longer were making the necessary connections. Again, the spare engine came to the rescue because it had a starter switch. Although that switch was also non functional, the contacts inside the switch were not broken, and Rich was able to use them to repair the switch. Thank goodness for the spare engine.

Promoting the adventure had taken a back seat to work on the Maxwell, but Rich did find time to reach out to the AACA museum curator, Stan Sipko to find out if they would be interested in a loan of the Maxwell for an exhibit after the trip had completed. Doug thought it would be nice to display the Maxwell after the trip was over for other people to enjoy. The AACA Museum was a natural choice. After a week, the response came back that the museum was not interested at this time because their space was extremely limited.

With the start of the trip a month away Doug and Rich talked about who would actually be going. The original plans were to take three vehicles and six drivers. Folks who earlier expressed an interest in going began to drop out. Tony, the engine builder was getting married and the timing of the trip would prevent his participation. Besides Doug and Rich there was only one other definite partner, and that was John Brasca. John, a retired police officer, expressed an interest in this trip from the beginning. His own dream was to take a cross-country trip, so this adventure was his answer. John was a resident in Massapequa on Long Island, about fifty miles west of Doug's house where the Maxwell was kept. Ricky Principi, a huge supporter from the beginning was pumped up about going but the reality was he had other business irons in the fire that demanded his time. Ricky thought he would travel with the boys for the first two days then turn around and return. Jimmy Waters and Rich Pisacano were in similar situations. It looked like those three would not be making the full trip. It was up to Doug, Rich, and John to undertake the entire journey. This meant despite all the great work done on the motor home by Jeff to prepare it for a cross-country trip, the team would only take two vehicles the distance, the Maxwell and chase truck with a trailer.

The progress continued on the Maxwell as the pieces came back together. John drove out regularly to help Doug and Rich. John and Rich removed a couple hundred staples and tacks that held the old canvas top to the frame. Once it was removed it was taken to Rob, so he could use it as a pattern to cut the new vinyl once it arrived.

Three days after getting the engine, the boys were ready to marry the engine to the transmission. Jay came over that evening and with his knowledge and skills, the transmission and clutch were attached in probably half the time it would have taken Doug and Rich. Jay was a life saver.

Engine and transmission are reattached

It was October 7th when the engine with the transmission was put back into the Maxwell chassis. It took three guys to maneuver the combination into place. Doug, Rich and John lifted, twisted, jiggled, and lowered transmission to get it past the firewall and into the drive train tube. The next two days the three of them worked on the wiring, clutch and brake pedals, instrument panel/fuse box, battery box, radiator installation, fan belt and starter switch.

On October 10th enough was done to attempt the first engine start. With video cameras running the engine came to life. The sound was music to their ears, even if it was a little rough. Before the boys could take it out on the road, a replacement floor board had to be cut and fitted into place. The following day, with the floor board in place, the Maxwell was taken out for its first test drive. It was exciting to see the Maxwell go up and down the street on its own power. Each trip was with different passengers cheering and honking the Klaxon horn along the way. As fun as it was, it was obvious to Doug and Rich that it needed fine tuning adjustments. It lacked power, and the engine had a bit of a gallop. Doug also noticed an oil leak around the oil pan. The Maxwell was running but the punch list of things to do was growing as new issues were uncovered. One of the head bolts was leaking water, and they needed to figure out how to adjust the carburetor for a smoother ride. However, the good news was that the Maxwell was back on the road, moving under its own power.

Jim Fetten stopped over one day to update the Maxwell cowl signage. Originally, Rich and Doug told Jim the Newark to San Francisco time was 11 days but with a little more research it was actually 11 days and 16 hours. To stay true to the car, Jim stopped over and updated the signage.

Jim does some fine tuning of the messaging

Rich returned to Austin in mid October after a thrilling marathon of the Maxwell's preparation tasks. One evening while out participating in some Texas social dancing, Kathy Hirsch, a friend of Rich's, mentioned how she had seen articles in the Wall Street Journal by A.J. Baime about old cars and the story behind them. Kathy suggested to Rich that he ought to reach out to A.J. and see if there was any interest in the story. Rich emailed AJ, and his response was nearly immediate. Rich and AJ connected up on the phone and much to Rich's delight AJ was thrilled about the story and wanted to do a photo shoot and write an article on this adventure. They planned on doing the photo shoot on Long Island when Rich returned in November.

Rich was re-invigorated after his trip to Long Island to find specific locations of Grandpa's pictures. Rich reached out again to the Lamar Chamber of Commerce in the hope of identifying the location of a picture Grandpa had taken while passing through Lamar. The initial attempt to contact the Chamber back in March using their "Contact Us" link had gone unanswered. The desire was to find out exactly where the Savoy Hotel was located in 1916. This particular photo was of Grandpa standing next to the Maxwell in Lamar, Colorado.

C.W. Tuthill outside the Savoy Hotel

The picture clearly shows the "Savoy Hotel." Rich asked the Chamber of Commerce and the Colorado Historical Society if they could help him identify the location of this picture. This time Rich used the Colorado Historical Society Facebook page. The Historical Society confirmed there was such a business in 1916. The owner was, C. L. McKittrick but no address. They suggested contacting the Lamar Public Library. A special lady there named Sheri Eirhart took our quest to heart and did some research looking at old maps. Sheri followed up with the local "Big Timbers Museum." The curator of the museum, Kathleen Scanton, found an old ad for the Savoy Hotel in a high school yearbook. The ad did not mention a street address but did say it was 1 block north of the Santa Fe Station. Using Google maps Rich looked at the street view of Main Street just north of the railroad station. Rich found

"Mike's Main St. Sports" shop that had a vague look of the building behind Grandpa. Rich called "Mike's" and talked with one of the employees there. Rich asked if their shop was ever next to the Savoy Hotel in 1916. They did not think so, but they took Rich's number and were going to check with an old local patron and let Rich know. Rich never heard back from them but a day later he got an email from Kathleen with a picture of the Savoy Hotel in 1921. It was on the west side of the street. Rich revisited Google maps this time looking on the west side. Where the Savoy had once stood was now West Poplar Street, but on the corner was K's Ceramics, which was undeniably the same building behind Grandpa in the photograph. Rich made note of the address for another photo opportunity on their planned route.

While Sheri and Kathleen were looking for the location of the Savoy Hotel, Rich took on another challenge. It was to find the location of another one of Grandpa's photos, but this one had no obvious landmarks like a hotel name. All Rich had to go on was Grandpa's hand-written note on the back that read, "cliff dwellings outside of Flagstaff".

Grandpa at the cliff dwelling

A Google search led to the Walnut Canyon National Monument. It was established by the US Forest Service then transferred to the National Park Service in 1934. Rich used their "Contact Us" link and made contact with one of the park rangers, Kyle Andersen. Kyle said he would circulate the photo to the staff and rangers to see if anyone recognizes the location. A day later, Rich got an email saying their lead archaeologist recognizes the location where Grandpa was standing in a "New York minute." That was great news, but Rich was also told that area was closed to visitors. The boys could only view the site from a public trail that was part of the National Park. Still Rich made another note for a photo opportunity when they were close to Flagstaff.

Rich was two for two and thought about a third picture Grandpa had taken at the Grand Canyon. Maybe there was a ranger that would recognize the location. Rich used the Grand Canyon Association Facebook page. Rich noticed they had that day posted a picture that had a background that looked remarkably like Grandpa's picture. Rich about fell off his desk chair thinking what a coincidence. Could the picture in the posting actually be that same spot of Grandpa's picture? Rich immediately posted a comment about their posting explaining the remarkable similarity to Grandpa's picture.

Grandpa and Scull at the Grand Canyon

The association responded within a day and told Rich it was not the same spot. The association, however, did say they would see if they could determine the location where Grandpa and Scull were standing. Unfortunately, that was the last Rich heard from the association but that didn't bother Rich, and he still added another photo opportunity to the route agenda.

53

Back on Long Island, Doug swapped out the carburetor. The Maxwell was now fitted with a KD carburetor. It was Doug's understanding that this style of carburetor was what was originally in the Maxwell. Using this carburetor allowed the adjustment of the fuel mixture from inside the cab.

Rob had finished making the new top for the Maxwell. So Doug took the Maxwell over to Rob's house so it could be fitted on the frame. Rob did a great job on the top. By the end of the day, the Maxwell had the new top in place ready for any bad weather the boys might encounter.

The GoFundMe account was growing thanks to the supportive donations from friends and family. This was relieving the financial burden of the trip. The Mattituck Laurel Historical Society likewise was very generous with their donations so the boys decided to add, "Mattituck Laurel Historical Society" to the spare tire cover provided by Coker Tire.

Maxwell ready for road testing

As October progressed, Rich worked on items on the punch list he, and Doug created before he left Long Island. Using Amazon and eBay resources, Rich tracked down things like the head light and tail light bulbs, engine temperature sensor, connectors and more importantly a backup ring gear. A fellow Maxwell owner and website follower, Howard Dennis, in Georgia had a ring gear. Howard's knowledge of Maxwells was a great source of information. He had a second ring gear for his own Maxwell. These gears are extremely hard to find and cannot be re-manufactured easily (or economically). Howard offered to send us this precious part to use if we had a ring gear failure. If we had to use it, we agreed we would buy it from him since a ring gear failure would have been a show stopper. Words cannot express the gratitude of this gesture. Howard's contributions did not stop there. He also contributed to this effort with 1916 technical documentation on the KD Carburetor and Atwater Kent ignition systems for Maxwell cars. These documents provided valuable operation and adjustments information. That information enabled the boys to do fine-tuning of timing and fuel mixture to help the Maxwell run smoother with more power.

With less than a month before departure, it was clear there would only be three men for the entire trip, Doug, Rich and John. Ricky, Jimmy, and Rich Pisacano still planned on joining the trip but only for the first day. Ricky offered up his Chevy shop truck for the chase vehicle and Doug decided to use the trailer that came with the Maxwell. This added work to the punch list because the trailer needed new tires as well as fixing a few electrical issues with the trailer lights. The boys also added a black paint job for the trailer to the punch list.

The use of the Chevy shop truck was a terrific contribution from Ricky. It resembled an emergency vehicle with multiple doors along both sides for storing tools, oils, sprays, additives, straps, and supplies for the trip. The inside of the truck left ample room for an array of spare parts. Axles, transmission, fan parts, brake parts, anything, and everything Doug had collected over the years. There was no telling what might fail. No one wanted to regret leaving a needed part at home. Having lots of space in the back of the truck allowed the boys to take a lot of spare parts.

The only problem with the Chevy was that it was fitted with two bucket seats. Not a problem going west because one or two would be in the Maxwell. However, the return trip meant all three boys would have to ride in the cab. Their solution was to put in a folding metal chair in between the bucket seats. This sounded like a workable solution, but they were soon to find out the disadvantage of the extra seat even though they fitted it with a padded lamb's wool cushion.

The October issue of the AACA Speedster came out, and the boys were thrilled to see their adventure in that newsletter. It was called "History Repeats Itself (Part1)" and included one hundred-year-old pictures of Grandpa and Scull. Stacy, the newsletter Editor asked for the Part 2 article to be written when the boys returned from the adventure.

It was not until the end of October when events took a turn for the worse. Not only did the engine leak oil around the oil pan, but it developed a significant leak around the distributor drive pulley spraying oil all over the engine compartment. Doug had to pull the radiator back out in order to investigate the issue. Using the spare motor as a reference Doug found a misplaced washer that was allowing excess movement on that pulley and shaft. Doug fixed the problem. Once again, it was a blessing to have that spare engine for reference.

In addition to the oil leak, Chevron delivered more disappointing news with an email telling the boys they were not "accepting unsolicited sponsorship, funding request, grant applications or project proposals." Both boys realized they missed the point that this was not a fund raising activity but a marketing opportunity for them. Although this was disappointing news, it was not totally unexpected. Their corporate insider, John Harper, stopped communicating with them. Whatever enthusiasm that John might have had at the start had, for some reason, evaporated. Although it was not the answer the boys wanted, they looked on the bright side. They would not be bound to buying just Texaco gas and oil products or subject to outside requests or marketing demands.

As October came to a close the activity on the website showed a huge increase in visitor traffic. The website had 471 visitors and subscribers almost doubled at 77. It was encouraging to see the increase. Many sent comments wishing they could experience the same adventure. The GoFundMe account had grown to over $2000 in donations.

Rich's plan was to return to Long Island on November 9th a week before departure, but sitting in Austin and not being around to help because he was 1,800 miles away was more than he could take. Rich booked another flight out to Long Island on November 2nd. This time it was just a one-way-ticket. Where and when Rich might return to Austin was up in the air.

On November 3rd the very next day; he was helping Doug reassemble the Maxwell after fixing the oil leak around the distributor shaft. Once that was done the focus was to improve the tuning of the car so it would run smoother and have more power. With the KD carburetor and technical specifications for both the ignition timing and the carburetor adjustments, the boys were confident improvements could be made. In the course of setting and adjusting the timing, the Maxwell was started multiple times. In the process of repeated starts the starter switch failed. The engine would not crank. Apparently the copper contacts inside the switch had broken just like they did back in October. The boys were concerned over this switch. They had enough spare parts to make one more repair, but if the switch failed again en route, they would have a bigger problem. They needed an alternative method for cranking the Maxwell's engine that was more reliable.

What they decided to do was to bypass this elaborate switch. They installed a twelve volt battery with a modern starter solenoid that could be activated with a push button. Luckily, this battery fit nicely under the front seat with the two existing six volt batteries. Since the Maxwell did not have the means to charge the twelve volt battery, they would take along a battery charger and charge it up in the evening while en route, if necessary.

Their alternative worked well, but it took a bit more coordination by the driver to start the Maxwell. First, they would have to push the starter pedal to engage the starter motor with the engine with right foot, simultaneously push the new starter button on the dash with the left hand, while working the throttle, spark advance and choke with the right hand. Doug got very good at this ritual. Some might even think it was comical watching Doug's starting routine.

The following day the boys got back to tuning the Maxwell. Using a timing light they were correctly able to position the spark advance so the control on the steering column would give the correct movement between advancing and retarding the spark. The Maxwell was definitely running smoother. A third piece of the floor board was cut from new wood and fit into place. Although they were anxious to do more road testing, the boys decided to drop the oil pan to fix the leak around the pan's gasket. Once the pan was off and cleaned there were obvious ripples in the mating surface. Using the oil pan on the spare engine might be a better choice so that oil pan was removed from the spare engine. Apparently, the oil in the spare engine had been there for some time because when Doug looked on the inside of the oil pan, it had an inch and a half what could best be described as a combination of molasses and peanut butter. It took a putty knife to scrap out the old oil. Although the oil pan had a flatter mating surface, there were pin holes in the bottom of the pan. Doug would need to use the original oil pan after all with a healthy dose of gasket sealer.

With the oil pan reinstalled, Doug and Rich then connected up the choke and the lean/rich control rod to the carburetor. With only a week before launch the Maxwell was back on the road for some more road testing. It was the first time they could get a feel for just how fast the Maxwell would travel. Without pushing it hard, Doug found it would easily go between 35 and 40 MPH. It was driven down to Jamesport Auto to get its New York State inspection, then to Waterview Terrance to take June for a ride.

On November 6th, just 10 days before the planned departure, Doug got an email from Doug Johnson. He just happened to be cleaning out his desk draw and found the article from Old Cars Weekly he had put in his desk six years ago. There was an exchange of emails with Mr. Johnson offering any help that might need in the Indianapolis area. Little did the boys know they would be taking Mr. Johnson up on that offer.

Folks subscribing to the website were asking about the planned route time line, so they would know approximately when the boys might pass through their town. The boys thought if they could average 30 MPH and drive ten or eleven hours a day, that would allow them to do 330 miles a day. At that rate, in ten days they should be able to complete the 3,100-mile trip a little faster than Grandpa. Using those estimates as a guide their timeline looked like this:

Day 1 - Newark, NJ to Laughlintown, PA - 320 miles

Day 2 - Laughlintown, PA to New Paris, OH - 327 miles

Day 3 - New Paris, OH to St. Louis, MO - 321 miles

Day 4 - St. Louis, MO to Emporia, KS - 358 miles

Day 5 - Emporia, KS to Lamar, CO - 380 miles

Day 6 - Lamar, CO to Santa Fe, NM - 330 miles

Day 7 - Santa Fe, NM to Springerville, AZ - 297 miles

Day 8 - Springerville, AZ to Grand Canyon, AZ - 253 miles

Day 9 - Grand Canyon, AZ to Needles, CA - 240 miles

Day 10 - Needles, CA to Los Angeles, CA - 286 miles

Using the online tools on his AAA account, Rich built a trip tik that identified the route down to specific road names and turns even though he imagined the route could easily change once on the road. It was not going to take long for the boys to realize just how hard it was going to be to stay on this schedule, which allowed no time for roadside repairs or breaks.

With the Maxwell back on the road going through some road tests it was time to pay some attention to the support vehicle and trailer that would be coming along on the trip. The boys picked up Ricky's Chevy shop truck to get it ready for the trip. The Chevy had no trailer light connector, so they had to wire up a trailer connector. Ricky also picked up yellow hazard lights for the trailer and the Chevy. The trailer got a new set of tires and a quick paint job changing it from a rusty orange to a flat black trailer. The final touches included a repair of the trailer's electrical wiring and the addition of two orange flags on the very back of the trailer.

Trailer gets a paint job

On November 10th, less than a week away from launch the sun was out in full force. It was a cool day with great expectations for the boys. This was the day the boys would be meeting with the Wall Street Journal photographer, Gordon Grant, for a photo shoot at the Hallockville Museum Farm. A.J. Baime, a Wall Street Journal reporter had arranged for the photo shoot. A.J. told Doug he would follow up with a phone call interview for his story.

John drove out from Massapequa that morning. The sky was blue with not a cloud in the sky with temperatures in the forties, perfect for an outdoor photo shoot. The three hopped into the Maxwell for a two-mile drive to the Hallockville Museum Farm to met Gordon Grant. It was a sampling of the cold weather they would be experiencing. They were joined at Hallockville by Lori Tuthill Yastrub, a C.W. Tuthill granddaughter, June and Maria, Doug's wife. Gordon spent over an hour taking pictures of the Maxwell from all angles, as well as pictures with Doug, Rich, John, and June. Gordon made them feel like celebrities. Gordon finally wrapped up with some actions shots of the Maxwell on the move.

Wall Street Journal photo shoot

The following day meant more road testing. Doug noticed that the distributor shaft was moving in and out as if it had an additional unwanted play back and forth accompanied by a clunking sound. Once again, the decision was made to pull the radiator and timing cover to add a second washer that came from the spare engine. Once again that spare engine came to the rescue. While the engine was apart getting the additional thrust washer, Kelly Zegers from the News-Review / Suffolk Times stopped by for an interview and a story for the local paper. It was a delightful session which included a video interview with Doug and Rich. The boys would not see the story in print until their return. After the break for the interview, the boys went back to work on the Maxwell. Besides the addition of the thrust washer, Rich worked on the throttle and spark advance linkages as well adding a brake light to the Maxwell. Back in 1916, this Maxwell had a tail light but nothing to indicate the driver was actually braking. The boys thought the addition of a brake light was a necessary safety precaution.

Later that day, Doug received an email from Karen Santos, who works for Jay Leno's car collection, called BGD Garage saying she was unable to accommodate the request for a visit. Apparently earlier phone calls with Jay's secretary were interpreted as a request for an invitation to Jay's collection by Karen. All Doug was asking for was a chance to share Grandpa's story with Jay. What looked like a sure thing after talking to GT Joey, the chance to meet Jay Leno in Los Angeles appeared to have fizzled out.

By November 12th, the Maxwell was back together and on the road again for more road testing. The oil pan leak was fixed, and no more oil was coming out from around the timing shaft. The play in the distributor shaft was gone. The Chevy van was fitted with caution lights. The trailer had new tires on and was painted. After months of planning and work, an on time departure from Newark looked good.

Sunday the 13th was a day to load up the Chevy support truck. The plan was to leave for Newark on Tuesday so that bright and early Wednesday morning, November 16th the adventure would start exactly 100 years from Grandpa's start.

The Team's "tool box"

The nice thing about having the Chevy van was there was ample space for almost every tool the boys had on hand as well as boxes of parts, oils, sprays, and gas additives. The spare transmission was taken even though second gear was badly worn. A front axle, spare brake shoes, old radiator fan, rear end housing and boxes of loose parts all labeled in zip lock baggies. Not knowing what challenges they would face the boys figured it would be better to take a part and not use it rather than needing that part while on the road. They even took a spare gas can that held twelve gallons of gas in case of emergency. The boys chuckled over the difference between what they were taking and what their Grandpa took, a single tool box on the running board.

June was busy with an idea of her own: she painted 14 gold stones with markings on both sides. One side had her father's initials, CWT with the year 1916 and on the flip side she put the initials of her two sons, DTB, RTB with the date 2016. Each stone was numbered. June suggested the boys leave these stones, one in every state, as sort of a bread crumb trail.

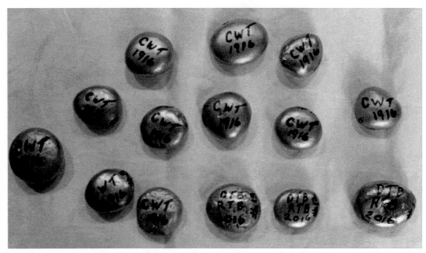

June's golden rock contribution for the trip

That night before leaving for Newark on the 15th, Rich looked at the activity on the website. With the adventure ready to start the list of subscribers to the website went into triple digits with a total of 101 subscribers.

With years of planning and preparation, the trip was about to begin. It was also a time to reflect on all the work and support from many folks to get to this point. Contributions of time, technical advice, money contributions, and personal time from many folks, the boys realized this was truly a team effort. They coined the phrase, "Team Maxwell" and added lettering on the trailer to recognize the broader support of a team of people all helping recognize Grandpa's accomplishment. From here on out it was Team Maxwell making this trip.

Chapter 4 – The Trip

Author's Note: *All entries from the diary of C.W. Tuthill will be worded and spelt exactly as taken from the diary. No additions or corrections will be made to that text. The term 'Therm' refers to the temperature at that time of the day in either the CWT diary or the Team Maxwell entries.*

November 15th was a cold damp day with rain showers expected for most of the day. The boys loaded up the Maxwell in the morning on the trailer that proudly was named, "Team Maxwell." The excitement of what they were about to undertake was exhilarating. The cold, wet weather did not hamper their spirits at all.

Loaded up for Newark, New Jersey

The plan was to trailer the Maxwell to Newark, New Jersey. Doug and Rich would pick up John in Massapequa. They would stay at the Robert Treat Hotel, just a block away from 544 Broad Street, the planned starting point. Ricky Principi, Rich Pisacano, and Jimmy Waters decided not to spend the night in Newark. Instead, they planned to leave Long Island at 2 AM in the morning, so they would get to the hotel in Newark by 4:30 AM. They would follow along for the first day then turn back for Long Island as Doug, Rich and John continued west.

The ride west on the Long Island Expressway was not difficult. It was 11 AM, and the worst of the rush-hour traffic had subsided. John had suggested they all eat lunch at his house before pushing on to Newark. The Newark

Historical Society asked to meet the boys that evening at 5:30. There was plenty of time for lunch at John's. John had a great spread of sandwiches and salad. With full bellies, they headed back to the Chevy bound for Newark. With all three in the cab, it was the first test of the folding chair between the bucket seats. With Rich in the middle seat his head would touch the roof if he sat up straight, but with a little lean forward, he had a clear view of the Chevy's hood and about twenty feet of the highway immediately ahead of them. No problem though, Newark was only a couple of hours away.

The historical society location was situated right next to the Robert Treat Hotel where the boys would spend their first night. The hotel was downtown just a block away from 544 Broad Street where the adventure would start. Although it was conveniently located, parking presented a problem. The hotel parking was not designed for a truck and trailer. The parking attendants found room that almost put the trailer on the sidewalk. Doug slipped the attendant a twenty in hopes he would pay a little extra attention to the Maxwell. It was dark already, and the Maxwell was covered up and locked down. Although no one said it, all three guys were hoping the car would be there safe and sound in the morning.

Doug, John, and Rich barely had time to take their bags up to the room before they had to head out to meet with the Newark Historical Society. The Society location was in the same block as the hotel. It took ten minutes to walk to their office. They were greeted by Steve Tettamanti, Greg Guderian, and Doug Oxenhorn, who showed them around the multiple floors that made up the Newark Historical Society. They had a friendly chat about Grandpa and the pending adventure. By eight, they were done and headed across the street for a meal at Blaze Pizza. After dinner, it was back to the hotel for a good night's rest.

CWT diary entry Day 1:

Thursday, November 16, 1916. Therm 50 Weather Clear **Started from Newark 7:30. Phila 12 o'clock Gettysburg 4:30 Arr'd at Pittsburgh after some high climbing at 1:20. Had lunch and went within 17 miles of Wheeling and slept outdoors. Had supper at Chambersburg.**

Team Maxwell Day 1:

Wednesday, November 16, 2016. Therm 45 Weather partly cloudy

Ricky, Rich, and Jimmy arrived outside the hotel at 4:30 AM after leaving Long Island in the wee hours of the morning. The Team collected in the hotel lobby. It was still dark when they left to walk around the block to the parking lot. Although no one said it, there was a sigh of relief when the team found the Maxwell, the chase truck, and the trailer right where they were left. All wheels were accounted for, and nothing had disappeared over the night. The Maxwell was uncovered, straps holding the Maxwell to the trailer were removed, trailer ramps put in place, and the batteries were connected. After a couple of attempts, the Maxwell sputtered to life. There was no stopping Team Maxwell now!

Doug backed the Maxwell off the trailer and pulled it out of the way along the curb. The trailer ramps were secured back on the trailer. Safety lights were turned on and put on the trailer fenders. Much like a parade, the Chevy pulled up behind the Maxwell followed by Ricky in his SUV.

The morning dark was giving way to daylight as Doug and Rich lead the parade from the hotel parking lot around the block to 544 Broad Street. This was the address of the Maxwell Dealership where Tuthill and Scull worked and where they had started their trip 100 years ago. The moment was captured in a flurry of photographs, and the trip began. Steve and Greg from the historical society were there to send the Team off on their adventure.

Ready to depart from 544 Broad Street

The Team decided that to avoid morning traffic they would get on the road early and look for a place for breakfast after getting a couple of hours into the day's trip. The sun came out, and the weather was cool but comfortable. The traffic was heavy with morning commuters. The team worked their way south on US 1 for 43 miles and at 8:30 stopped at the Corner Bakery Cafe just south of Princeton. After a delicious breakfast, the oil was changed in the Maxwell there in the Cafe parking lot. Because it was a newly rebuilt engine with a few hours on it now, putting in fresh oil was the right thing to do. Doug also drained the oil in the wet clutch and to his surprise drained two and a half quarts of oil out of the clutch that should have only had a pint of red transmission oil. Oil apparently was making its way from the crank case to the clutch. This was not something that could be fixed on the road so the team decided to keep an eye on oil levels at every stop.

Rich left behind gold stone #13 in the Cafe parking lot and Team Maxwell was back on the road by 10 AM after adding gas and fresh oil. Doug and Rich were riding in the Maxwell enjoying the sunny weather, honks, and waves of the passing cars. The Team traveled south on US1 as the morning sun was rising higher. Rich looked to his right and saw the sun was casting a silhouette of the Maxwell and two men against the road bank. Rich taped Doug on the shoulder and pointed to the shadow. "Look, Grandpa and Scull are riding with us!" Future coincidences gave the boys the distinct impression Grandpa and Scull were looking out for them.

Looks like C.W. Tuthill and P.G. Scull are with the Team

An hour into the trip Ricky pulled up alongside the Maxwell at a traffic light and Jimmy rolled down his window and yelled, "Your rear left tire appears to be wobbling." As Doug pulled away from the light, he noticed the Maxwell did, in fact, have a bit of a shimmy. Doug and Rich pulled into the Faulkner Hyundai dealership and drove the Maxwell towards the back lot. The Chevy with John and Ricky in his Tahoe paraded behind the Maxwell. Once stopped the problem was obvious. The left rear tire split the side wall and the fifty five pounds of air pressure on the tube inside was bulging out. The folks at the dealership shop came out to see what was happening and offered help. The bad tire was replaced with the only spare that was brought while Rich called Coker Tire and made arrangements to have a new tire shipped ahead to Bob Larimore in Springfield, Ohio. Bob was the Maxwell owner the Team planned on visiting. The spare tire was installed in minutes, and the Team was back on the road.

The Team crossed into Pennsylvania by 12:30 PM and picked up Route 30 West. They were done with New Jersey. Rich looked at Doug and said, "One state down, eleven to go." But the next state was expansive Pennsylvania: it would be a while before the Team was done with state number two.

The Maxwell was running well and logged 107 miles by 2 PM. The Team pulled off Route 30 for another gas stop. This time the Maxwell gas tank was filled to capacity, which was eight gallons. Before pulling away Rich noticed the Maxwell was dripping fluid from the steering column. It took one sniff to realize it was gasoline. It was running down the steering column, but why? Since the boys had never filled the gas tank completely before they did not realize the tank had a hole on the upper half that was allowing the gas to run out, down the tank, over the floor board and along the steering column. Pulling out the gas tank was not an option so for the next two hours the aroma of gasoline was with the Team. Needless to say this was not helping the Maxwell's gas mileage. From then on the Team would only put four to six gallons of gas in the Maxwell at a time.

As they progressed west on Route 30, the weather started to change. The sun had given way to clouds. The Maxwell was running well maintaining a 30-35 MPH pace. Not the fastest car on Route 30 but not the slowest either. It was along Route 30 when the Team experienced a first. They passed another vehicle! That is if one considered an Amish horse and buggy another vehicle.

The clouds got heavier and darker eventually leading to rain just outside of Lancaster, PA. With just 138 miles into the trip, it was time to put up the Maxwell top and side curtains. Doug pulled off into a Walmart parking lot and he and Rich raised the top and buttoned the side curtains while Ricky and Jimmy picked up some Wendy's burgers and fries. It was 3:30 PM before the Team was back on the road pushing on through the rain.

First rain on the Lincoln Highway (Route 30)

Thankfully, the rain did not last and once west of York, PA the Team pulled off again but this time to take the top back down.

Driving with the top up created a bit of a problem because it meant Doug and Rich had to hunch over more. Without the top, there was more head room making the drive more comfortable. Grandpa was six foot two and that probably explained why in most of their pictures, they, too, drove with the top down. It was 5:15 PM when the rain stopped and appeared that it was not coming back so the top was put back down and the side curtains stowed under the back seat. It was getting dark. The Team had only logged 185 miles at this point. This was a far cry from their 330 mile goal for day one.

Driving in the dark posed another issue. The headlights were not the brightest. The fact that they pointed high and to the right did not help with the visibility. With still over 100 miles to meet their goal the decision was to sandwich the Maxwell between the Ricky's Tahoe in front and John with the Chevy warning lights flashing in the back. The Team pushed on in this formation. By 6:00 PM they reached Gettysburg but kept pushing west. The Maxwell needed gas by 6:30 PM and it was at this point the Team decided trying to drive in this formation was difficult. As much as they were hoping to make Laughlintown, PA at the 330-mile point, it was not safe. Plus half the Team had been up since 2 AM and was reaching the point of exhaustion. They called ahead and found a hotel in Chambersburg, PA. By 7 PM, the Maxwell rolled into the Country Inn and Suites in Chambersburg. They had logged 225 miles the first day and after only one day were behind Grandpa's pace. The Maxwell was covered, the Chevy truck buttoned up, and the Team headed off to the Texas Road House for a late dinner where Rich left another "golden rock" before returning to the hotel.

End of Day 1, Maxwell covered for the night

CWT diary entry Day 2:

Friday, November 17, 1916. Therm 35 Weather Snow Got up at 7:30 Had breakfast at Wheeling left there 8. Had accident with sheep at 8:30 Cost $8.25! Had dinner Columbus and supper at Eaton, O. Made Indianapolis 1:15 Stopping at Hotel Oneida. Broken fan, leaking radiator, loose steering. Made

802 miles to here. Sent cards home & H., Mr. Porter & Mr. Parrish. W. Va & Ohio

Team Maxwell Day 2:

Thursday, November 17, 2016. Therm 43 Weather sunny

In reviewing Grandpa's dairy the Team realized that Chambersburg, where they stopped, was where Grandpa had supper before continuing on their journey on day 1. Grandpa and Scull did not stop during the night until they were just east of Wheeling, West Virginia. The Team estimated they were close to 200 miles behind Grandpa. The Team was chasing Grandpa, right from the start. With clear skies and cool temperatures, the Team was optimistic for a good day of driving that would enable them to gain on Grandpa or at least not lose any more ground. So they thought.

After breakfast in the hotel, the Team uncovered the Maxwell and went through their pre-start rituals. They again found over 2 quarts of oil in the wet clutch. Two quarts of oil where there should have only been a pint and a half. It was obviously engine oil that was still seeping into the wet clutch. A pint of fresh transmission oil was added to the clutch, and the engine oil was topped off. The floor boards were pulled up and the gear box oil was checked. It was at a good level. With all the oil levels checked and the Maxwell started, it was time to start the day. Ricky, Jimmy, and Rich had decided this would be as far as they would go. From here on out it was up to Doug, Rich, and John to finish the journey.

The Team is ready to start day 2

Ricky headed east on Route 30 while Doug, Rich and John continued west on Route 30 with expectations of logging 300 miles or more on this sunny day. The cool and sunny weather was ideal for a drive in the Maxwell. Engine heat passed under the floor boards and into the cab, adding extra warmth for the boys' feet. Add in the long underwear and ski pants made the ride comfortable. In order to get their 300 miles today it would be necessary to average 35 miles per hour. Not hard for today's cars, but the Team soon put the Maxwell to the test going up the mountains, just west of Fort Loudon. The Maxwell ran well on all four cylinders but that 24 horsepower engine could only muster 25 MPH, sometimes even slower as it tackled the Pennsylvania Mountains. It was a slow ride up the winding Route 30 two-lane road with very little shoulder. On the plus side, there was not a lot of traffic so the slow pace did not result in a long line of cars following the Maxwell.

It was a good test for the Maxwell. Doug thought the clutch might be slipping so they stopped to give the Maxwell a bit of a rest and give the Team a chance to check oil levels. Rich switched places with John and climbed into the Chevy van while John hopped in the Maxwell with Doug. The Team pushed on up the mountain. It was not long before the uphill climb turned into a downhill rush. Rich felt a short term sense of relief as he followed the Maxwell downhill. Down a narrow, winding road with very little shoulder and steep drop offs. Turns were marked with huge signs posting truck speed limits of 20 MPH and giant black and yellow arrows. Many turns were blind turns some as sharp as ninety degree turns, which prevented a view of oncoming traffic. Rich was praying the oncoming traffic was staying in their lanes. Now instead of doing 25 MPH coming up the mountain the Maxwell wanted to go 40 MPH and faster. This was not the road to do 40 MPH, maybe if riding with James Bond in his Aston Martin but not in a 1917 Maxwell.

It was not long at all before Rich noticed a slight plume of smoke from the passenger rear tire. It quickly grew into a definite white stream of smoke. Honking the Chevy horn, he tried to get Doug and John's attention. With the breeze in their face and the smoke trailing behind them, they did not realize what was happening. The smoke turned into billows of white smoke as Rich continued to honk and flash the truck's lights. The wooden wheels had been soaked in kerosene and linseed oil on the advice of other car owners to keep the wood wheels from drying out and splitting. If the brakes got hot enough, a tire fire was entirely possible. Although the Team had a spare tire, they had no spare wooden wheel. It would be the end of the adventure. Fortunately, Doug and John heard the racket behind them and quickly found a place where they could just barely get off the road. Rich and the Chevy could only get partly off the road. A crisis was avoided, and the Maxwell's brakes got a much-needed rest.

Much-needed stop to let the brakes cool

Once back on the road Doug used second gear a lot more down the rest of the mountain with no more brake smoke. At 9:30 AM, Doug and John pulled over into a vacant gravel parking lot. The sun was out, and the weather was nice so the Team decided to drain and refill the clutch oil after that grueling test up and over the mountain. They also pulled up the floor boards, so they could get to the clutch inspection plate and adjust the clutch hopefully to correct the slip Doug felt going up the mountain. The procedure for adjusting the clutch tension was not difficult. It basically meant having to equally tighten three bolts that can be seen through the access panel under the floor board. With the clutch adjusted and fresh oil in the clutch the Team was back on the road by 10:30 AM. They crossed over the Sideling Hill Summit on the Blue Ridge Mountain and stopped for a photo opportunity at an elevation of 2195 feet.

Over the Pennsylvania mountains

After traveling another thirty miles the Team reached Bedford, PA. It was here that the Maxwell engine had developed a tapping noise. Doug pulled off the road to investigate. Not sure where the noise was coming from, Doug called Tony the engine builder for advice. Although Doug was able to send Tony a video of the running engine, it was difficult to diagnose. Tony suggested a valve adjusting locking nut might have worked loose. The decision was made to operate on the engine to inspect the locking nuts on the valve adjusters. This required removing the carburetor and intake manifold in order to get to the valve adjuster cover panel. The weather was still sunny and comfortably cool so the operation began. It took a significant effort to remove the panel and finally get to the valve adjusters. None of the locking nuts were loose, but the gaps were larger than what was called for in the Maxwell instruction manual so Doug proceeded to readjust the valve clearances.

With the engine parts spread out on the ground, a passerby stopped and asked if the boys needed any help. The gentleman was Jim Diehl from Shiny Nickel Customs just two miles away. Some may say it was luck, and others might say it was divine intervention but Jim's arrival was a blessing. Doug was having a problem adjusting the valves. Doug needed a thinner open end wrench to do the valve adjustment. Jim left and came back with a wrench to enable Doug to adjust the valves. Jim left, and the Team promised to return the wrench once done but Jim insisted they keep the wrench should we need it again. Gratefully, the Team took the wrench not realizing that it would be needed again.

Roadside adjustment of the valves

All in all, this stop took three hours of daylight before the Maxwell was back together and back on Route 30 west towards Wheeling, West Virginia. It would soon be dark and with less than 100 miles logged so far, it was evident that they would not catch up to Grandpa today. The reality is that the gap between them, and Grandpa was widening. They were still chasing Grandpa.

The original goal was to be in Wheeling, West Virginia before dark. Jeanne Finstein, a member of the "Friends of Wheeling" wanted to arrange for an antique car escort across the 1849 Wheeling Suspension Bridge. The same bridge Grandpa would have taken in 1916 but now was a historic landmark with strict traffic rules ever since a heavy Greyhound bus used the bridge causing some damage. Rich reached out to the Friends at Wheeling and explained the delay. Clearly, the Team would not make Wheeling before dark. The idea of an escort over the bridge sounded great but was not at all likely. However, Jeanne Finstein and Joanne Sullivan were still anxious to meet the Team and see the car across the bridge. They asked to be kept informed as the Team approached Wheeling.

It was close to 5 PM when it was getting dark, and the Team decided for safety sake to load the Maxwell on the trailer and head to Wheeling. Calling ahead to Jeanne and Joanne the Team made plans to meet in the parking lot of the Knight Inn a block before the suspension bridge. They would then unload the Maxwell and even though it would be dark, drive it across the suspension bridge just like Grandpa.

The Team arrived at the Inn by 7:30 PM, and was happily greeted by Jeanne, Joanne and others. Their warmth and excitement to see the Team was not dulled by the late arrival. After introductions and a quick recap of the day's events, the Maxwell was unloaded. With Jeanne in the front with Doug, John and Rich took up a seat in the back. With the GoPro camera running the Team drove over the suspension bridge, just like Grandpa did 100 years ago. The bridge was old and sturdy, clearly a product of 1849 engineering. Once crossing the bridge Doug circled back for a return trip over the bridge and around a block of downtown Wheeling.

Across the suspension bridge with Friends of Wheeling

It was a delightful visit with the Friends of Wheeling. Jeanne gave the Team a tour of the Robert W. Hazlett house that was just two blocks from the suspension bridge. It was a house Grandpa most likely passed as they approached the bridge. Also noted was that the Team approached Wheeling through a tunnel into downtown. A passage not available to Grandpa in 1916, as the tunnel was built in the 1960s. Grandpa would have actually had to go not through the mountain but around it on Route 40 or what was known in 1916 as the National Old Trail Road.

After leaving the Hazlett house it was back to the Maxwell. Loaded on the trailer the Team decided it was time to push on towards Springfield, Ohio. The engine noise was still present after adjusting the valves. Bob Larimore and his Maxwell were in Springfield. If they could make there by the end of the night, they could visit with Bob in the morning and get his input on the engine noise. Plus Bob had received the spare tire and tube from Coker Tire that needed to be picked up.

The Team made it to the Marriot Courtyard around 10 PM after a less than exciting meal at Bob Evans. They had connected up with Bob and planned on driving to his Coachworks shop first thing in the morning. Grandpa had spent the night in Indianapolis. Grandpa had about a 130 mile lead on Team Maxwell even though they had an accident with a sheep. By the end of day two the Team was still chasing his pace.

CWT diary entry Day 3:

Saturday, November 18, 1916. Therm 50 Weather Fair

Staid at Indianapolis. Went to Texaco station and got gas. Worked on car Went to presto-o-lite service Left town 10. Had dinner at Terra Haute, Drove into night, Sent cards in A.M. Had supper at Vandalia. Slept outside of St. Louis in the car. Ind & Ill

Team Maxwell Day 3:

Friday, November 18, 2016. Therm 63 Weather Sunny

Anxious to meet with Bob, the Team skipped a breakfast at the Marriott and headed directly over to Bob's Coachworks shop. Bob met the Team there with his 1917 Maxwell. After checking out Bob's Maxwell the Team talked about the engine noises the Maxwell was experiencing. Bob was super gracious and offered the full use of his shop's bay and tools. Unfortunately, Bob would not be able to stay as he was off to a car auction. After some thought, the Team decided they would not use Bob's shop and continue west on Route 40. Bob did send the Team off with a new set of sparkplugs, and a spare clutch should they have a clutch failure. The spare parts were loaded into the Chevy along with the new tire and tube sent to Bob by Coker Tire.

Twin Maxwell photo opportunity

The Team left Bob's shop and realized breakfast was long overdue. As they navigated back to Route 40, they stopped at a quaint local diner called "Mel-O-Dee" for a terrific brunch. Rich left golden rock #2 in their parking lot. It was approaching 11 AM before the Maxwell was unloaded and prepared to start that day's run. Not a very early beginning for day three. Grandpa had left Indianapolis an hour ago and was increasing his lead on Team Maxwell.

On the plus side the weather was incredible: sunny and approaching the 70 degree mark. Route 40 was a pleasant road to travel. With two lanes of flat straight road, it was a stress free drive. The Team was not holding up traffic because there was ample room for cars to pass. Although the engine noise persisted, the Team continued west on Route 40. They crossed into Indiana a little before 2 PM with four states down and only eight more to go. By 2:30 PM, after 76 miles of delightful driving, they arrived in Cambridge City, Indiana. Driving through Cambridge City they came upon a huge mural of Abraham Lincoln depicting his memorial funeral train. Last year, April 30th, 2015 was the 150th anniversary when the funeral train passed through Cambridge City on its way to Springfield, Illinois. It was a definite photo opportunity so Doug pulled up in front of the nation's 16th president!

Stop at Cambridge City Lincoln mural

While parked under the watchful eye of Lincoln, the Team discussed what to do about the engine noise. Doug called Jeff back on Long Island and described the issue. Since they had already checked the valve adjusters, the second assessment was that it could be a possible exhaust leak. At first, the Team thought they would work on removing the exhaust manifold once they got to a hotel. Then the thought occurred to them to reach out to Doug Johnson, the gentleman who just days ago contacted Doug in response to the article Doug wrote six years earlier. Doug Johnson was located in Indianapolis, less than sixty miles away. In addition, weather reports were issuing warnings of a coming cold front, and rain was expected.

Doug gave Doug Johnson a call, and he responded with an absolutely positive response. He even offered to come out and get the Maxwell. That was not necessary, it was explained that the Team could easily trailer the Maxwell to his shop before it got any later. It was a great plan. Under the watchful eye of the Lincoln mural, the Maxwell was loaded up and the Team made a bee-line to Mr. Johnson's shop. Rich left behind golden rock #14 at the base of the Lincoln mural.

They arrived at Doug Johnson's shop before dark. The temperature was already dropping, and the wind was picking up. As they pulled up to the shop door, they were greeted with a swat team of car know how. After brief introductions, the Chevy with trailer and Maxwell pulled into a huge shop. The Maxwell was rolled off the trailer and within thirty minutes, the swat

81

team found the location of an exhaust leak. Once again, the Maxwell engine was partially disassembled so the exhaust leak could be corrected to prevent any valve damage. After discussing the earlier valve adjustments it was decided to readjust the valve clearances to match, not the old specs but newer specs since the engine was rebuilt with newer valves. This was all possible in the warmth of the shop. Outside the predicted rain storm pummeled the shop roof with strong winds. The Team was tremendously grateful for not just the technical help but the convenience of a dry place to work. No way could these changes have been made in a hotel parking lot during the storm!

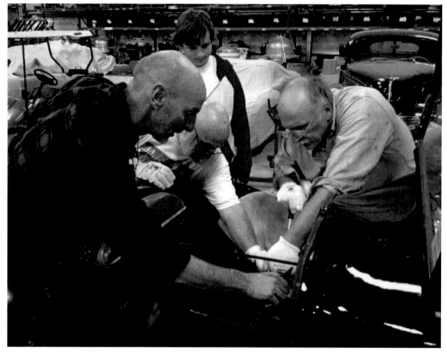

Identified the exhaust leak at Doug Johnson's shop

By the time the Maxwell was reassembled, Doug Johnson suggested leaving the Maxwell in the shop in favor of a visit to his project garage. This garage was a dream man cave for any car enthusiast. His shop housed several performance car projects in progress, along with lots of automobile memorabilia. He had an incredible passion for high performance and speed. The Team was mesmerized by the recounting of Doug's racing stories.

The evening concluded with dinner at the Olive Garden and a stay at the Hilton Garden Inn at Indianapolis. By the end of day three the boys realized

Grandpa had stretched his lead. While Team Maxwell stayed in Indianapolis, Grandpa had spent the night just outside of St. Louis, Missouri. His lead was now 250 miles, a full day of driving. Grandpa was still being chased and the Team marveled at the pace he and Scull were able to achieve.

CWT diary entry Day 4:

Sunday, November 19, 1916. Therm (not recorded) Weather Fine

Drove into St. Louis at 9:30. Had lunch at Thompson and found Mr. Hopkins took him to oil station where we filled with gas oiled up etc. Had dinner with Mr. Liponer of Texas Co. Left St. Louis –3 P.M. After getting mail. Ferry across Missouri at St. Charles. Stuck for ferry at Boonville at midnight. Put up until A.M.

Team Maxwell Day 4:

Saturday, November 19, 2016. Therm 38 Weather morning snow flurries

After a hotel breakfast, the Team headed over to Doug's shop to pick up the Maxwell and start the day's journey. The weather had changed dramatically in the last twenty-four hours; not just the drop in temperature but a strong wind that cut right through their clothes. It was a definite morning for the long underwear. Before 9 AM the Maxwell was picked up and ready to start a cold day of driving.

Ready to push on with exhaust leak fixed

The Team decided to trailer the Maxwell to Route 40 rather than leaving right from shop. This avoided Interstate traffic and saved some time. Doug Johnson lead the Team out of town with a stop at AutoZone to restock on transmission oil for the clutch, bearing cups for the trailer and a new bulb for the Chevy brake light which apparently blew out earlier on the trip. An additional purchase was made that Rich thought was odd. Doug picked up a tire repair kit for fixing tubeless tires (not Maxwell tires). Rich asked Doug, "Why the repair kit, Doug?" and Doug just answered, "Ricky does not have one for the Chevy, so I thought it would be good to have it with us." Looking back on that purchase Rich thought it was Grandpa who planted that suggestion with Doug, because it would be needed.

The Team picked up Route 40 just north of the Indianapolis International Airport. They pulled into a convenience store parking lot to unload the Maxwell. On that particular morning it was a challenge getting the Maxwell started. Doug went through his usual ritual of setting the spark advance, throttle position, adjusting the rich/lean setting, pulling the choke, pushing the starting pedal with his foot while depressing the start button on the left side of the steering column. It took quite the coordination effort along with timing to manipulate so many engine controls. Anyone who has started a car this way can appreciate the convenience of cars today that can start with the push of a single button. Despite Doug's best efforts the Maxwell did not cooperate. The starting battery was losing power and fingers were getting cold just as a snow flurry had started. The Team resorted to rolling the Maxwell off the trailer and next to the Chevy for a jump start. The combination of the extra energy from the Chevy jump and a few squirts of starting fluid coaxed the Maxwell into making encouraging sounds. The effect of that starting fluid eventually solved the problem. Once the Maxwell started and warmed up a little it was ready to start the day's trip. By 11 AM, the Maxwell was back on the Route 40 heading west. The snow flurries subsided.

Route 40 was a straight divided highway with light traffic making the ride delightful even though it was still quite cold. With two lanes in each direction, the Team did not worry about holding up any traffic as they kept a 35 MPH pace. Frequently, the Team would pass National Old Trail Highway (N.O.T.) signs. These signs indicated where there were still parts of the original National Old Trail road. It was almost noon when they approached Reelsville, Indiana that they decided it was time to check on one of these N.O.T. roads. The one at Reelsville ran parallel to Route 40. Doug pulled off Route 40 and

84

drove down this original part of the N.O.T. They realized it could very well be the same road Grandpa rode on. It was a single-lane road lined with trees and grass on both sides. If two cars had to pass one would need to drive on grass. The road consisted of well worn and cracked concrete. In 1916, it probably was dirt. The road led to a bridge across a small river bed.

Driving part of the original National Old Trail Road

It was a thrill to believe this bridge could have been used 100 years ago by two Maxwell salesmen on a cross-country journey. It also gave cause for one to reflect on what the actual roads were like 100 years ago. They were not divided highways, but narrow probably dirt single lane roads. Despite this fact, Grandpa was still a couple hundred miles lead on the Team.

The Team reached the Illinois state line after traveling 70 miles. Another state, Indiana, was in the books, with only seven more states to go. It was close to 1:30 in the afternoon when the Team crossed into Illinois. They were now on central standard time (CST) and gained another hour. The Team was excited about this because it would give them another hour of daylight driving. The temperature was holding at 37 degrees with cloud cover as they rolled into Casey, Indiana. The clouds gave way to the sun as the afternoon rolled on.

When they got to Toledo, Illinois, they took another detour. This time it was to go over the Cumberland County Covered Bridge. The bridge is a Historic National Road Art and Architecture site. The bridge had been safely designed and rebuilt to carry modern-day cars and trucks but was built on the same site as the original covered bridge. Another moment to reflect on Grandpa's journey was the crossing over the original Cumberland Bridge.

The rebuilt Cumberland County covered bridge

After recording a video of the Maxwell with Doug and John passing over the bridge, the Team continued west on Route 40. It was another hour and half of driving before the Team came upon a road side flea market that looked like a great place to stop and check the Maxwell's oil and stretch their legs. It was almost dusk but "Gregory's Flea Market" could not be passed up. Surely there would be untold treasures there, maybe even some Maxwell touring car memorabilia.

Like many flea markets, there were multiple vendor booths with everything from golf clubs to kitchen utensils. The Team decided on a mission. Among the tables of old games, broken toys, signs, clothes, and untold items for sale, they decided to look for a kitchen measuring cup. Every time gas was added to the Maxwell it was accompanied with some lead additive. This was a suggestion from multiple antique car drivers. Every gallon should get a half an ounce of lead additive. Not having any proper measuring device the lead additive was approximated. Having a measuring cup would help improve the accuracy of this task. While searching for such a measuring cup they passed many shot glasses. In a flash of inspiration, they realized a shot glass that is meant to hold an ounce of liquor would be perfect for their needs. A shot of lead additive for every two gallons added to the Maxwell. The proprietor, Gregory who was participating in the search gave the shot glass to the Team.

The sun was starting to set, but the Team was having fun exploring the different vendor booths. As they wandered about, Rich came upon a display of model cars. To his amazement, on the shelf was none other than a C.W. Tuthill and P.G. Scull toy Maxwell.

Discovery of Grandpa's toy bank

What were the chances? Rich immediately took the model up to the front checkout and informed the cashier that the car in the box was out in the parking lot. Of course, she was amazed and wanted to know the story behind the trip followed by a walk out to the Maxwell. The boys offered to autograph the toy but in all the excitement never actually did that. As it was, in the Chevy, the Team had seven of the same models all autographed by June Tuthill Bassemir.

The stop at the flea market lasted longer than anticipated but Doug bought a great old wooden Allis-Chalmers box. Doug was not sure what he would use it for, but the old, well worn box with the Allis-Chalmers logo was a conversation piece. The Team stayed at the flea market chatting with Gary until the sun had set. The flea market was closing up and it was time to move west. Since it was dark, the Maxwell was loaded back on to the trailer after a great day of driving and adventure.

The Team looked at their route and decided to trailer the Maxwell to a Holiday Inn Express in Vandalia, Illinois. From there the Team figured they could make St. Louis, Missouri to drive across the Eads Bridge in the late morning. By the end of day four Grandpa and Scull were just east of Boonville, Missouri waiting on a ferry. Grandpa was over two hundred miles ahead of Team Maxwell. They were still chasing Grandpa.

CWT diary entry Day 5:

Monday, November 20, 1916. Therm 65 Weather Fair

Left Boonville at 9 o'clock reached Kansas City I P.M. 125 miles. They fixed the car at the Maxwell service station and we got away at 6 P.M. Passed thru Emporia at midnight. Slept at night between Emp & Hutchinson. Mo – Kansas

Team Maxwell Day 5:

Sunday, November 20, 2016. Therm 27 Weather sunny

With 27 degree temperature, the morning was sure to be a cold one. Doug was sure to put on the long johns and Rich put on not just long johns but his ski pants as well. The Team had breakfast at the hotel which included a one-button pancake maker. A clever device where all one has to do is depress one button and in about two minutes, a golden-brown pancake slips off a conveyor belt. It had to be the easiest way to make a pancake. Rich left golden rock #10 in the parking lot of the Holiday Inn.

The Team decided before the day started it would be wise to stop at Walmart in town for a few items they thought they would need. Doug wanted a warmer pair of gloves, and Rich decided the ski cap was nice but a hat with side flaps would be a welcome addition, even if it meant the fashion Gods would frown on him. While shopping at Walmart, Doug spotted a small American flag that could be mounted on the Klaxon horn.

In the Walmart parking lot, the team changed the engine oil, the clutch oil and mounted the American flag on the bracket that held the Klaxon horn. Doug also replaced the spark plugs and checked and adjusted the points. John added Team Maxwell decals to the left side of the trailer. Up until now, only folks on the passenger side would see the Team Maxwell signage. With John's addition, everyone passing the Maxwell trailer would see the Team Maxwell signage, and there were a lot of folks passing the Team.

Preparing for the start of day five

With all the shopping done, prep work completed and a stop at a gas station, the Team was back on Route 40. It was already 10:30 AM by the time they were on the road. It was cold but hardly a cloud in the sky as the Maxwell puttered along towards St. Louis, Missouri. St. Louis was 70 miles away so they figured they would get to St. Louis before 1:00 PM.

The Team crossed the Missouri River on the Eads Bridge just like Grandpa, although the bridge undoubtedly has seen some updates. They crossed Illinois off their list as they entered Missouri. Six states were down, six more still to go.

Crossing the Eads Bridge into St. Louis

With the information from Emily at the Missouri Historical Society, the Team progressed down Washington Ave and worked their way through downtown St. Louis towards St. Charles. It was Sunday afternoon, and the city roads were not heavy with traffic, but many lights meant a lot of stops and starts for the Maxwell. It was slow progressing through St. Louis. They had hoped to stop in to see Emily to thank her for her help in planning the trip through St. Louis, but their schedules did not line up.

The Team stopped at a Wendy's in Bridgeton for lunch before progressing towards St. Charles on Route 180. Rich left behind golden rock #8 in the Wendy's parking lot. Not wishing to get on the Interstate with the Maxwell the Team planned a route around St. Charles on US 370, which turned out to be as busy and fast as an interstate, but once past St. Charles, they followed side roads that paralleled Interstate 70. It was slow traveling but an easier and safer drive than tackling the interstate. It was almost 5 PM when they approached Wentzville on Pitman Ave. The Team stopped under the interstate overpass in a commuter parking lot. Just to the north of them was a General Motors Assembly Center.

Looking at the route ahead the Team could see it was mostly interstate roads. The sun was starting to set so they decided to load the Maxwell on the trailer and head for Boonville. They booked a room at the Boonville Holiday Inn Express and had a great dinner at the town's Cracker Barrel Restaurant.

A recap of the day's travels revealed to the Team they may have made Boonville by the end of day five, but Grandpa started his day from Boonville and was now past Emporia, Kansas. Grandpa still had a good 200 mile lead as the Team continued to chase him.

CWT diary entry Day 6:

Tuesday, November 21, 1916. Therm 45 Weather Fair

Filled up with oil at station 30 gals. Went across farm prarie land starting 10 A.M. Had a country dinner at only restaurant at 1:30 St. John. Pushed on thru Dodge City & stoped just this side of Lamar & bunked in. Had supper at Dodge City. Kansas & Col.

Team Maxwell Day 6:

Monday, November 21, 2016. Therm 29 Weather sunny

Before the Team left the hotel, they looked at the day's route. The Route 40 they had been following so far was one in the same with Interstate 70. Wishing to avoid the high speed traffic, trucks, and stress of Interstate driving they mapped out alternative roads that ran parallel to I70. Although these roads were better suited for a 35 MPH Maxwell, it was not the most direct route and often switched back and forth over I70. Some roads were labeled "Old Highway 40." Other roads were just labeled with letters like "M,", "Z," and "AE." It took a bit of careful planning because some of the roads dead ended. If not careful the Team would have had to back track to continue west.

After a couple of "one-button button pancakes" at the hotel breakfast, the boys bundled up and headed out to uncover the Maxwell and prepare it for the day's journey. Rich pulled out golden rock #3 and left it at the Holiday Inn Express entrance.

A blanket of cold air settled over the Maxwell and the car had a bit of a problem starting. As usual, Doug would try starting the Maxwell while it was still on the trailer right there in the hotel parking lot but this morning it was just not cooperating, as if to say, "I am not starting until it gets warmer." Eventually, the twelve volt cranking battery was losing enough energy to crank the engine fast enough for a start. Not to be denied the Team rolled the Maxwell off the trailer. The Holiday Inn Express was on a hill, and the boys were going to try and push start the Maxwell. There was a convenient hill that led from the hotel down to a Caterpillar Industrial building at the bottom. Down the hill Doug rolled, popped the clutch, the Maxwell coughed, sputtered, started and then stopped. Doug came to rest at the bottom of the hill smack in the middle of the Caterpillar employee parking lot.

The Chevy van pulled up alongside of the Maxwell. Out came the jumper cables. The extra kick from the Chevy's battery was enough to overcome the cold and start the Maxwell. It was 9 AM, and the Team was ready to hit the road to start the day's adventure. The morning temperature gave way to warmer weather as the sun rose. It became a beautiful sunny day just right for a casual drive west, on side roads. The objective was to get to Kansas City for lunch with an old friend John Raffel, who was waiting for the Team's arrival.

About an hour into the westward journey the Team once again passed an old, weed infested side road and building that begged them to stop and check it out. Further investigation revealed the building had no markings but there was evidence of an old car lift. By peaking inside the windows one could see a single large room cluttered with an abandoned washing machine, riding lawn mower and old tires. The Team speculated it might have been a service station at one time because of two wide garage door openings that were boarded up to keep out any undesirables.

Photo opportunity at an old service station

92

As the Team left they could not help but wonder if Grandpa and Scull had seen this building. Maybe even stopped and visited.

Fifty-five miles later while traveling on the North Outer Road, another attraction caught Doug's eye. This time it was not an old road, a dilapidated building, or even a historical marker. It was a junk yard with an assortment of old vintage cars. For three old car junkies, this was too good to pass up.

Doug turned the Maxwell into what appeared to be a private driveway, up a slight incline and stopped next to a single-story ranch-style house. They were greeted by a man with a dark blue down jacket, yellow work gloves, and a ball cap that read, "Free men don't need permission." His name was Dick and welcomed the boys to his place. After explaining the journey the Team was on, they asked if they could walk the yard to see what cars were there. Following the driveway that Doug pulled into, they continued via a dirt and grass path to the back yard where they entered "Tricky Dicky Junk Yard."

The Team wandered around the well weathered and rusted cars in various forms of health. Cars laid on the ground, while others had missing hoods, broken windows, and rotting tires. Each vehicle had their own story of years past and their own adventures. It was not long before the boys realized why there was a reason for stopping at this graveyard of cars. It was a 1949 Chevy with missing front wheels, rusted roof, and aged trunk, but most of the glass windows still intact. The shiny trim around the windows was a sharp contrast to the brown rusted fenders. This car was significant to Doug because back on Long Island was Doug's own 49 Chevy. Although Doug's Chevy was road worthy and running it was in need of some parts and this looked like an ideal donor.

The hood was lifted off to reveal an empty cavity where an engine once powered the Chevy. Now it was long gone. A metal tube that the average person would pay no attention but, was recognized by Doug immediately as the duct work used to funnel air from the front of the car into the inside. These are not easily located and when found not in as good of shape as this one. "What would you want for that?" Doug asked Dick. Dick proceeded to tell the story of a man that wanted to buy the whole car but never returned and did not call back. Dick agreed to sell the air duct to Doug. John went back to the Chevy and drove it into the junk yard pulling up next to the 49 Chevy. The shop truck had all the tools, and sprays needed to free the tube from the engine compartment.

Stop to pick up some spare parts (not for the Maxwell)

After an hour wandering Dick's junk yard and salvaging much-needed parts the Team headed west once again. They were about 30 miles east of Kansas City and John Raffel an old friend of Rich's was waiting to connect up with the Team and grab a Bar-B-Q lunch. They met with John on the outskirts of Kansas City and followed him to the well known local spot.

It was already 2:30 in the afternoon when John and the Team pulled up to "LCs Bar-B-Q" famous for its tender meats and frequented by Kansas City football players. The smell of barbecued ribs and brisket was delightful. The inside counter was in front of huge fire pits where meat was cut and plated for the patrons. The dining area had a scattering of a dozen small tables and the walls were filled with framed pictures of sports memorabilia and BBQ awards. A roll of paper towels sat in the center of every table. John treated to the Team to a smorgasbord of meats; brisket, turkey, sausage. The home-style fries were incredible and the hungry Team savored every morsel. There's nothing better that eating local cuisine with friends.

Lunch at LC's with big supporter, John Raffel

This meal was a highlight of the trip and one that would be talked about for the rest of the trip. After an hour of gorging, it was time to get back on the road. The Team wanted to get to Newton, Kansas before the end of the day and daylight was running out.

John led the Maxwell and Chevy van through the Kansas City suburbs, eventually they turned left on to State Line Road. As they traveled south on State Line Road, Missouri was on the left and Kansas on the right.

The Team drove until dark and loaded the Maxwell on the trailer in Emporia, Kansas. It was a good day of driving with over 200 miles covered. With the Maxwell on the trailer, they drained the warm clutch oil out and replaced it with a fresh pint of transmission fluid and topped off the engine oil then headed to Newton, Kansas.

The Team stayed in Newton that evening at the Holiday Inn Express without eating any dinner. The lunch at LCs was so filling no one was hungry. They realized they had completed passing through state number seven and had five more to go, but Kansas was a long state. They faced at least one full day of driving before getting to Colorado. They also realized that Grandpa was "bunking in" as he put it in his diary, just outside of Lamar, Colorado. Grandpa had stretched his lead on them to over 300 miles. Perhaps they spent too much time at that old service station, or at Tricky Dicky junk yard, or maybe it was eating at LC's that afternoon. However, the Team did not regret any of those stops and looked forward to tomorrow's adventure as they continued to chase Grandpa.

CWT diary entry Day 7:

Wednesday, November 22, 1916. Therm 10 Weather Fair

Breakfast at Lamar after freezing the radiator coming in town. Sent cards had dinner in La Junta. Arrived in Trinidad 4:45. Took on 30 gallons of gas at the Texas station and went to bed after a bath. Some sleep. Colorado

Team Maxwell Day 7:

Tuesday, November 22, 2016. Therm 56 Weather sunny

When the Team got up at 7:30 AM, it was raining lightly and the weather did not look favorable. After the "one-button button pancakes" and some hot coffee, they walked to the parking lot to uncover the Maxwell. The water proof cover, not being a tight fit, sagged in the middle where it collected a few gallons of water from the night rain, but on the bright side, the clouds were traveling eastward and a glance to the west was laced with blue sky. It looked like it was going to be a clear drive west. Rich left golden rock #1 in the Holiday Express parking lot by the fire hydrant.

The Team headed west on Route 50 towards Dodge City, about 170 miles away. The clouds disappeared, and the sun came out before they even left Newton. They filled the Maxwell with two gallons of gas and one shot of lead additive. Then they added another eight gallons to the spare gas tank in the Chevy as well as topping off the gas in the Chevy shop truck. They were on Route 50 heading west in with the sun shining by 9 AM.

The roads were flat and straight just as Grandpa described as prairie and farm land. There was not a lot of land mass to block the strong cross winds that whipped across the sides of their faces. Rich imagined the side wind might have been as strong as their 35 MPH head wind. It was just a two-lane road with a 65 MPH speed limit but thankfully not a lot of traffic. The occasional east bound tractor trailer that passed the Maxwell sent a blast of air that pushed the car towards the road's shoulder. Thankfully, Route 50 had a smooth wide shoulder so the Maxwell had room to move to the right for the following cars to pass when needed. Doug would honk the Klaxon horn when passing cattle and they would slowly glance up while still chewing a mouthful of grass. No doubt they were thrilled to see us pass, and if they did not have their mouths full, they might have even answered the Klaxon.

Two and a half hours later and 76 miles towards Dodge City, the Team made a gas stop for the Maxwell in Stafford, Kansas. The sun was still shinning, and high forty degree temperatures were pleasant for driving. By 12:30 PM, they had traveled 100 miles and pulled over to check oil levels in the Maxwell. The Maxwell was running well. All along the road laid bright yellow/orange corn grain as if a transport truck lost a sack or two of corn kernels and scattered these down the highway.

Stop to check the oil level on the way to Dodge City

The consumption of the LC's lunch and the hotel breakfast was finally wearing off so the Team stopped in Kinsley for lunch at Strates Kountry Kitchen. With only 35 more miles to Dodge City, it was a great spot to stop, eat, and stretch their legs. Strates was a comfy home style dining experience with a friendly waitress and patrons. Oak tables sat in the center of the room and oak booths lined the walls. The Team slid into one of the booths and placed their orders with the waitress. One particular friendly gentleman in bib overalls, an obvious farmer, struck up a conversation about the Maxwell. The boys' order of burgers and fries arrived, and the farmer stayed and chatted up a storm. He made himself at home and slid into the booth next to John. All was going well and pleasant until the farmer's conversation drifted to stories of the local slaughter house. Not exactly the graphic stories the boys wanted to hear as they swallowed their burgers. By 1:30 PM, the Team was back on the road.

Tall windmills were scattered across the prairie but despite the wind, they stood their ground and did not move. Doug joked and asked Rich "How are the windmills and us the same?" When he was unable to come up with an answer, Doug supplied it: "Neither one is moving".

As they traveled west, they could see white billows of clouds on the horizon blooming like cotton balls in the distance. The temperature was quickly dropping. Along the way, they came upon the slaughter house mentioned by the farmer during lunch. The large building where the cattle were "processed" was surrounded by fields of cattle. The Team pulled over amazed to see hundreds if not thousands of black cattle wandering pastures around the building. None of the boys had ever seen so many cattle in one spot before. It was like looking at a school of minnows in the water. It was sad to think about the fate that awaited them. An hour later as the Team pulled into Dodge City the sun was completely hidden by the clouds and temperatures had dropped to the low 40s.

The Team agreed that Dodge City was not what they expected. Probably due to the fact they watched way too many western movies growing up. There was no dirt road lined with saloons, a blacksmith shop, and a sheriff's office. Instead, it was a typical town with Wendy's, Pizza Hut and a JC Penny's stores along the Route 50. It was not until the Team turned south down Central Street and headed to the Boothill Museum did they get the feel for the original "Dodge City." Next to the Boothill Museum was a replication of old Main street Dodge City. Just like in Bonanza or the Rifleman TV shows. Unfortunately, this was their off-season and no gun fights or variety shows were happening. Outside the Boothill Museum was an old locomotive engine which presented another photo opportunity for the Maxwell.

Dodge City Locomotive photo opportunity

The area looked more like a ghost town than a beehive of western activity. The Team wandered through the Museum gift shop then around the grounds as the temperatures continued to drop. They ran into a gentleman in a blue hooded sweatshirt and a thick bushy white mustache that looked like he was putting up Christmas lights on the locomotive. A maintenance worker perhaps? Nope, he was none other than the Marshal of Dodge City, Brent Harris, who just happens to lend a hand around the grounds during the off season. The boys were fascinated by the Marshal, who entertained them with stories of Dodge City and Wyatt Earp.

The Team visits with the Marshall of Dodge City

After an entertaining history lesson on Dodge City, the boys parted ways with the Marshal. With the sun setting and the temperatures approaching the thirties the Team decided to load the Maxwell on the trailer. They completed 170 miles on day seven in the Maxwell. Once on the trailer Doug and the Team performed what was becoming the evening ritual. Clutch oil was drained, fresh oil was added, and the engine oil topped off. Batteries were disconnected; the Maxwell was securely strapped down, and fuel shut off. It was time to get out of Dodge.

Tomorrow's goal was to get to Lamar, Colorado by lunch time so the Team decided on staying at the Hampton Inn in Garden City, Kansas. After arriving at the hotel and covering the Maxwell for the evening the Team walked over to Samy's Steakhouse for a delicious steak and potato dinner. It was another blessed day with cool but clear weather. They looked forward to visiting Lamar, Colorado. The Team reflected on the fact that Grandpa had already passed through Lamar by day seven and did not stop to sleep until he reached Trinidad, Colorado. Grandpa was well over 200 miles ahead of them, but that was better than 300 miles the prior night. They were still chasing Grandpa but gaining ground.

Rich went through his evening routine to update the website with a blog to recount the day's adventure. This particular evening was difficult because Rich could not establish an Internet connection with the hotel's WiFi. After multiple attempts, calls to the hotel front desk and a useless call to the service provider's help line Rich gave up and walked over to the IHOP next door. With a pot of coffee and their free WiFi Rich uploaded videos, pictures, and posted the day's blog. It was almost 2 AM when he returned to the hotel room. Doug and John were sound asleep.

CWT diary entry Day 8:

Thursday, November 23, 1916. Therm 30 Weather Fair

My Birthday 28 yrs. Left Trinidad at 7:30 Went over Raton Pass and across plains following Santa Fe R. R. to Las Vegas where we had dinner. Pushed on all night and passed through Albuquerque to Socorro Had supper at Santa Fe. Sent some cards. Col & N. M

Team Maxwell Day 8:

Wednesday, November 23, 2016. Therm 35 Weather sunny

It was Grandpa's birthday and if he were alive he would be 128 years old. The morning wakeup call came way too early for Rich. He was still in bed when Doug called out from the bathroom, "We have a guest." Doug was referring to a cock roach he killed in the bathroom. The thought of bugs on a transcontinental ride with the Team prompted them to inspect their luggage. Doug called down to the front desk. The hotel manager came up to the room while Rich was taking his turn in the shower. The manager apologized and refunded the cost of the hotel.

The outside temperature was 35 degrees so the Team dressed with long johns and snow pants. It would be another cold morning, but the Team was grateful to see more sunny weather. The original plan was to continue on Route 50 west, a very flat, straight two-lane road with a 65 MPH speed limit. Not a bad road for a modern car, but with very little shoulder, it was not the best road for a slow-moving vehicle. Before they left the hotel, the Team mapped out a route that would keep them off Route 50 as much as possible. They had roughly 100 miles between them and Lamar, Colorado. That would be roughly a three-hour ride. Because they would cross another timeline and enter into Mountain Standard Time they were sure they would be in Lamar in time for lunch.

By 8:30 AM, the Team was back on the road. Traveling on the back roads that paralleled Route 50 they used, Jones Avenue, River Road, and Route 25 to snake their way towards Lakin, Kansas. In Lakin, the Team picked up the original Santa Fe Trail. It was a hard dirt and gravel road that ran beside the Santa Fe Railroad tracks. It was flat, dusty and lined with short grass and cactus on both sides. An occasional tree sprang up, but for the most part, it was like riding on an old west wagon trail. It was thrilling for the Team to imagine 100 years ago it was highly likely Grandpa was on this very same road.

Riding on the Santa Fe Trail towards Lamar, Colorado

The Team took full advantage of the dirt road by exploring some of the joining cross roads. One such road took the Maxwell down to an old railroad bridge made of timbers from years ago. Another route revealed the "Indian Mound", a historical landmark used for navigation back in the 1800s.

After exploring these side roads the Team was ready to continue their western journey. The Maxwell, on the other hand, was not and stalled when they tried to restart it. Despite their best efforts, the Maxwell refused to start back up. When Doug cranked the engine, it would sputter as if it was only running on one cylinder. The Team checked the plugs and points as well as looking for the presence of gas on the plugs. It was baffling until they made an unusual observation. While checking to see if each spark plug was getting a spark Rich would hold the spark plug wire a half an inch from the top of the spark plug while Doug cranked the engine. No spark on plug one, and no spark on plug two, but a great spark on plug three. When Rich held the spark plug wire to the number three cylinder too far away for a spark the engine started! Granted it was only running on three cylinders, but it did start. When Rich connected spark plug wire three back to the spark plug, the engine died. What the Team found was inside the distributor was a carbon path from the number three terminal to the center post. This electrical path resulted in sending a spark to the number three spark plug every time rather than distributing the spark to the other spark plugs. The fix was easy. Cleaning the distributor cap removed that electrical path. Once that was done, the Team was back on the road heading to Syracuse, Kansas.

At noon, they stopped to fill up with gas in Syracuse and were pleased to find out they had crossed into Mountain Standard Time (MST), and it was only 11:00 AM. They were confident they would be in Lamar by lunch time. Forty minutes later, they crossed the state line and entered Colorado. Eight states were in the books and only four more states to pass through.

Just before 1:00 PM the Team rolled into downtown Lamar and headed right for the intersection of Main and Poplar. That was where Kathleen Scranton had identified the location of their next photo opportunity. When Grandpa stopped for a picture it was by a cafe and the Savoy Hotel. Now, 100 years later, the cafe was called "Kay's Ceramics". Instead of the Savoy Hotel being next to the cafe, there was Poplar Street. Apparently, the Savoy Hotel was taken down and replaced with a street. The Team wanted to capture a picture as close to the same one as Grandpa had taken 100 years ago. The problem was it was on Main Street with a near-constant flow of traffic. Stopping in front of Kay's would hold up traffic. Rich took up a position south of Kay's while Doug circled the block and took up a position just north of Kay's. A traffic light just north of their location provided them a window of opportunity. Doug pulled on to Main Street in front of Kay's, hopped out of the Maxwell and ran around to the front of the car, struck a pose with his hand on his hip like Grandpa, and Rich snapped the picture.

Grandpa in 1916, Doug in 2016, Main Street, Lamar, CO

From Kay's Ceramics, the Team headed north on Main Street (Route 50) to the Big Timber Museum just outside of downtown Lamar. Kathleen Scranton, the museum curator, was instrumental in helping the Team find the location of the Savoy Hotel. It was a delightful visit with Kathleen and her assistant curator Caro Hedge. The museum was filled with glass cases full of artifacts and memorabilia. The boys listened intently to Caro as she told the story of the Fleagle Gang. Ralph and Jake Fleagle along with two others robbed the First National Bank in Lamar in 1928. They were all eventually found and either killed or executed. Their case was the first ever in which a single fingerprint was used by the FBI as evidence leading to a conviction. It was good to know it did not happen when Grandpa was in town. Rich left a golden rock at the Big Timbers Museum.

The Team was feeling hungry and asked for a restaurant recommendation from the ladies at the museum. Kathleen suggested they try a home-town burger joint called "BJ's Super Burger". They headed back downtown to BJ's for burgers and fries. The inside of the restaurant had booths around the dining room, and each booth had what looked like the old-style juke box to play music, but instead you used that to order your food. By 3:00 PM, with full bellies the Team was ready to get back on the road but there was one more stop to make in Lamar.

On the way in to Lamar, just outside of downtown the Team made note of a junk yard. Now that they had something to eat it was time to explore it to see what treasures they might find. They back tracked slightly on Route 50 to stroll through the junk yard. Unfortunately this time there were no treasures to uncover so the Team hopped back in the Maxwell and Chevy. By 3:30 PM, they were once again heading west on Route 50.

Still with a couple of hours of daylight the Team pushed on in hopes of not losing any more time to Grandpa. By the time they got to La Junta, they had gone 170 miles, and it was too dark to continue in the Maxwell. They loaded the Maxwell on the trailer and headed for Trinidad, Colorado.

The Team headed southwest on US 350. It was about 80 miles to Trinidad. It was just a two-lane highway that stretched across the plains with very few towns, gas stations, or rest areas. The road was very flat and straight for most of the journey. This was unusual with all the mountains surrounding them. There was absolutely no shoulder and a 65 MPH speed limit. The Team was grateful not to be driving the Maxwell in the dark on a two-lane high speed road. It was on this road when Doug noticed the truck's battery light came on, and he saw the alternator was not charging the battery. Without the alternator charging, the battery would only be able to drive as long as it was strong enough to power the car's ignition system. With nowhere to stop the Team had no choice but to push on. Just shortly before reaching Trinidad Doug reported the battery light was out, and the alternator was charging again. Although that was a good sign, all three knew a total failure of the alternator could happen at any moment and strand them roadside. Perhaps Grandpa could use his influence to help them along.

The alternator on the truck continued to charge the battery when they approached Trinidad. At Trinidad, the Team made the decision to pick up Interstate 25 south and head for New Mexico. On the interstate, the emergency services would be easier to find than the back roads of Colorado. The Team thought they would try to make it to Las Vegas, New Mexico. It meant another 125 miles on Interstate 25, probably another two hours. They gambled the alternator would continue working. Part way to Las Vegas the battery light came on once again, but the Team kept going. After a few more miles the battery light went off again; and as if to toy with the Team the Chevy's alternator continued this pattern of failing and then working, failing then working. Clearly they had an alternator that was on its last legs. A complete failure was only a matter time. The alternator held on, maybe with some help from Grandpa, and the Team rolled into the Holiday Inn Express in Las Vegas, New Mexico at 8 PM. Thanks Grandpa. It was an exciting finish to a great day of driving, sightseeing and sunny weather. In the morning, the

Team would worry about the Chevy's alternator as there was nothing they could do at this point.

Once at the hotel, they reflected on their progress. They finished day eight in Las Vegas, New Mexico. They were done with state number nine, Colorado, just three more states to go. Grandpa finished his day just outside of Socorro, New Mexico. He still had a 200-mile lead on the Team as they continued the chase. The Team figured Grandpa would increase his lead tomorrow because they would have to solve the Chevy's alternator issue before continuing. Doug and John quickly fell asleep and Rich made the nightly blog update to the website with pictures and videos from the day's adventure.

CWT diary entry Day 9:

Friday, November 24, 1916. Therm 30 Weather Fine

Came in to Socorro at sunrise and had a good breakfast. Spanish in design went to Magdalina. Left there 10 A.M. For Sringerville. Arrived at 5 o'clock nothing between but plains, mountains & woods. Came in to St. John for supper. Put on to Winslow. Changed tires 5 times today. N.M & Ariz

Team Maxwell Day 9:

Thursday, November 24, 2016. Therm 44 Weather sunny

Thanksgiving Day, and the Team was thankful the alternator did not leave them stranded on the road last night. That morning they would have to correct the problem. Doug called Jeff at Jamesport Automotive back on Long Island, and Jeff's advice was to start the truck and disconnect the battery. If the car stops, the alternator is shot and would have to be replaced.

After breakfast in the hotel, Doug started the truck and disconnected the battery. The truck immediately stopped indicating that the alternator was bad. The question was, where would they find an alternator on Thanksgiving Day? The local AutoZone was closed. Doug did find an O'Reilly Auto Parts that was open and to his relief, they had a Chevy alternator in stock. As an added bonus, they were only four miles from the hotel.

Before the Team loaded up for O'Reilly Auto Parts, Doug noticed the left rear tire was nearly flat. The alternator did not fail last night, but the truck picked up a screw and the tire was going flat. The truck did not have a spare. They would have to find an open convenience store that offered air for filling tires. With a nearly flat tire and a failing alternator, they headed through town with all eyes looking for "air". They came up on an Allsup's Convenience Store with an air pump. They pulled the Chevy van with the Maxwell in tow up next to the pump before the tire was completely useless. A sense of relief was felt when they were able to find an air pump on a day when most stores were closed.

Of course with repair shops closed on Thanksgiving Day, the Team would have to spend a day in Las Vegas had Doug not had the forethought to pick up a tire plug kit at AutoZone three days earlier. The impulse purchase earlier in the week turned out to be a valuable decision. Unfortunately the tool was not the best quality. It broke while trying to use it to clean the hole in the tire. It was frustrating not just because it broke, but Doug bought the "better" more expensive tool that day. As one might imagine tempers were a little short. After the frustration at the quality of the "better" tool passed, Doug used a push drill to clear the hole and cleanly inserted a patch plug. After putting four dollars into the coin-operated compressor to fill the tire back up, the Team was ready to continue on to O'Reilly Auto Parts.

With just over 2 miles to go to the auto parts store they thought they had it made, but it was not a sure thing. Shortly after pulling out of the convenience store parking lot all the dash instruments lost power. In newer cars when the computer recognizes a problem with the battery charging circuit, it will shut down the instruments in an effort to save battery life. Still a half-mile from O'Reilly Auto Parts the truck lost power and would only go about five miles an hour. It was as if the Chevy was in a dessert and on its hands and knees, crawling towards an oasis. The truck kept moving but only as fast as a pedestrian could walk. The auto parts store was not yet in sight, but the Chevy was still crawling. It was like watching a video in slow motion as the Team drew ever closer to the destination. When the O'Reilly's sign was finally spotted, there was a collective sigh of relief, but there was one last hurdle to go: between the Chevy truck and the O'Reilly Auto Parts was a traffic light, and it was red! As they approached the light Doug declared his intention to run the light. They all believed if they let the truck stop on the highway, they would not get it rolling again and there would be no way to push the Chevy with trailer off the road. Just as Doug entered the intersection, the light turned green. (Thanks Grandpa) The entrance to the auto parts store parking lot was only a few hundred feet on the right-hand side. The vehicle turned into the lot and rolled up to the O'Reilly store front. They did not need to turn off the truck. It stopped all by itself as if to say, "I got you here, now fix me."

The folks at O'Reilly Auto Parts were super supportive. They put the Chevy battery on a quick charge and offered the Team any tools they needed. The clerk did not realize the Chevy was loaded with tools, but the offer was welcomed. The Team got to work on replacing the Chevy's alternator.

Chevy van gets a new alternator

As one might imagine the parking lot at O'Reilly Auto Parts was pretty empty on Thanksgiving morning. The sun was out with temperatures in the fifties which made working on the Chevy easier. The Team did encounter one passerby who looked at the Maxwell on the trailer and struck up a short conversation. The boys explained they were driving the Maxwell across the country. "Then what is it doing on the trailer?" was his response. The wise crack was not appreciated given the morning did not get off to a great start. However, the gentleman meant no real harm and handed Doug two twenty-dollar bills towards a Thanksgiving dinner. The Team figured because they were unshaven and dirty from working on the Chevy it must have looked like they were down on their luck. It was a nice gift and one they would use later in the day.

By 11:15 AM, the Chevy was back together with a new alternator and a charged battery. The battery light indicator was not lit, and they were ready to unload the Maxwell and continue west towards Santa Fe and Madrid. Rich left golden rock #9 behind in the O'Reilly's parking lot.

Before breakfast, the Team planned out the day's route after the Chevy repairs. Not wishing to drive on Interstate 25 meant finding side roads to get them past Santa Fe to Madrid, their next photo opportunity. Fortunately the Frontage Road 2116, Old Denver Highway, Route 50, and the Old Las Vegas Highway would keep them off the Interstate for all but 4 miles.

The Team traveled Route 2116 through Rowe east of Santa Fe. There were a few wispy clouds but not enough to block the sun light. The road was flat with fabulous landscape of rock formations and foot hills to their left. Straight ahead the mountains were rising in the horizon. They saw snow on the mountains tops.

It was 1:30 PM as the Team passed through Santa Fe. The temperature began falling but at 45 degrees, it was still warmer than the windy plains in Kansas. They were traveling on Rodeo Road to avoid the interstate traffic when Doug pulled off the road to do a check of the engine oil level and for everyone to stretch their legs.

Doug opened the hood and leaned an ear in towards the engine while it was still running. "Do you hear that?" he asked Rich. Rich also leaned in and tried to listen for what Doug was hearing. "It sounds like a whine." Doug said, but Rich did not pick it up. Doug was convinced something was wrong as Rich struggled to listen for the strange sound. Doug was definitely more in tune with the engine and varied the engine speed. He was confident the noise was coming from the radiator fan. They stopped the motor and took the fan belt off so the fan could freely spin. Without the other engine noises, a couple of spins of the fan was all it took to realize the bearings around the fan shaft were the source of the problem.

The boys removed the fan from the engine, so they could inspect the bearings, or what was left of them. The cage that held the tiny steel balls in place was totally destroyed. The tiny steel balls were all loose. The bearings needed to be replaced. This was not a part carried at any auto parts store. Normally, one would have to start searching on eBay and Internet antique parts suppliers. The Team looked in that spare engine box of parts they packed in the Chevy.

The fan from the spare motor was in the box, badly bent, mangled and totally unusable. However, the bearings on the fan shaft were just what the Team needed. Some may consider the fact they had this set of bearings as a stroke of good fortune. But after nine days of "strokes of good fortune" the Team believed Grandpa was with them, providing for, and protecting them.

There on the side of the road, they dissected the old fan to remove the usable bearings. The bearings from the old fan shaft were removed, heavily lubed with grease and installed in the existing fan shaft. The spare motor had once again provided a solution.

Replacing the radiator fan bearings

By 3 PM, the Maxwell was back together humming down Rodeo Road towards Madrid, New Mexico. It was less than 30 miles to this town. The Team was sure they would get there before dark. Madrid was where the "Wild Hogs" movie was filmed and reportedly the restaurant featured in the movie; "Maggie's Diner" was still there. The Team hoped to be able to take some photos at the diner before the sun set. An hour after fixing the fan bearings, Doug pulled off the side of the road. The Maxwell was running rough, so they stopped to check and clean the distributor.

It was just before 5 PM when the Team pulled into Madrid traveling down Main Street. The streets were empty. Shops were closed with not a soul to be seen. It was as if it was a ghost town, because it was Thanksgiving, the Team figured everyone was home for their individual turkey day traditions. Madrid was a one street town so finding Maggie's was not hard. They pulled up with the Maxwell for a photo opportunity.

A stop at Maggie's Diner (now a gift shop)

By the time they were done taking pictures it was after 5 PM. The hope was to have a Thanksgiving meal in Madrid, but with nothing opened it was time to move on. The sun was setting, and the evening was ushered in. Minutes later, the Maxwell was loaded up on the trailer heading towards Albuquerque about 45 miles away.

While they were on the road to Albuquerque, the Team scouted out a plan for day ten. Since it was a holiday, places to eat dinner were scarce. The Team settled for a Thanksgiving dinner at Applebee's in Albuquerque. At the dinner table, the Team decided to shoot for Socorro, New Mexico. They could pick up Route 60 at Socorro in the morning and avoid driving the Maxwell on Interstate 25.

After dinner, it was an eighty-mile drive to the Socorro Holiday Inn Express. It was not their most productive day in terms of mileage. The Chevy was running fine with its new alternator, but the Maxwell was still running a little rough with an occasional misfire. They would have to check it out in the morning in the daylight.

They arrived at the hotel before 9 PM and went through the nightly routine of draining the oil out of the Maxwell's clutch, adding new oil, shutting off the gas, disconnecting the batteries, and covering the Maxwell up for the night. Back in the hotel Doug and John did some laundry while Rich logged on to the Internet and reported the day's events on the website blog. According to Grandpa's diary, he drove all night and ended up in Winslow, Arizona by morning. The Team had fallen behind Grandpa by over 270 miles. They marveled at the pace Grandpa had set especially when they considered he did not have the benefit of paved roads. Clearly spending time fixing the Chevy did not help them catch up to Grandpa. However, it could have been worse because Grandpa also had problems this day. Grandpa mentioned that he had to change tires five times due to bad roads. The Team was grateful they had better roads and would not have to be changing tires. But they were still chasing Grandpa. Rich posted a blog of the day's progress while Doug and John fell fast asleep.

CWT diary entry Day 10:

Saturday, November 25, 1916. Therm [no notation] Weather [no notation]

Arrived Windslow 6:30 A.M. After all night drill had breakfast and pushed on to Flagstaff. Bad roads. Worked on car all P.M. As gasoline has not arrived. Sent cards etc. AZ

Team Maxwell Day 10:

Friday, November 25, 2016. Therm 36 Weather sunny

The day started out a chilly 36, but the forecast was to warm up into the 50s. The planned route for the day was to follow Route 60 west from Socorro to Springerville and hopefully make it to Winslow by the evening. Before breakfast, Doug connected up with A.J. Baime from the Wall Street Journal for an interview about the adventure. By 7:30 AM, the Team had their "one-button button pancakes," a cup of coffee, and were headed out to uncover the Maxwell for another day. Since the Maxwell was running a little rough Doug put in the new spark plugs that Bob Larimore from Ohio had donated. The

Team used what they learned earlier for cold morning starts. Giving a shot of ether into the engine it fired up faster with less cranking on these cold mornings. The new plugs made the difference. The Maxwell was running fine again.

Preparing for another day of driving

The Team stopped at AutoZone to pick up more oil and were heading west on Route 60 by 9:00 AM. Route 60 was a flat two-lane road with a shoulder wide enough for the Maxwell to make room for passing cars. There was not a lot of traffic, which made the driving easier. The sky was blue and cloudless as the Team drove through plains, forests and mountains just as Grandpa had mentioned in his diary. The scenery along Route 60 varied from flat plains with only bushes to outcroppings of rocks and hills. It was a scenic drive.

It was not long before the Team came upon the town of Magdelena. Grandpa had referred to it in his diary as a town with a Spanish design. It was a small town lined with sparse one-story buildings. Only a hint of Spanish style buildings was seen along Route 60. Outside of town were wide-open stretches of land that were very straight, and very flat with mountains on the horizon. The Maxwell passed by a line of large radio satellite dishes that were part of the National Radio Astronomy Observatory. An obvious addition since Grandpa passed through town. The Maxwell was running well, but Doug picked up on a new noise that seemed to be coming from the driver's side. It was a rattle that would happen at certain speeds. It was difficult to isolate because it was not consistent. They kept on driving.

After 140 miles of driving the Team reached the Arizona state line by 1:30 PM.

Crossing into Arizona

Crossing into Arizona meant the Team had traveled through ten states with just two more left. Arizona was a wide state though, and it would take them more than a day to cross it. Once in Arizona, the focus turned to finding a place to have lunch. They decided to look for a restaurant in Springerville just a few miles into Arizona.

They found the Safire Restaurant at 2:30 PM. They were pleased in completing 158 miles. Inside was a friendly waitress who served delicious Mexican food. Doug really liked the enchiladas; John and Rich cleaned their plates as well. From the booth where the boys sat, they could see one of the locals perched on a stool at the lunch counter. Strapped to his hip was a revolver. Obviously, Arizona was an open carry state. Doug said, "I want to move to Arizona." with a chuckle.

With their stomachs comfortably filled the Team loaded up and got back on the road. They picked up Route 191 north heading to St. Johns where Grandpa mentions in his diary he had supper. The City Hall building downtown looked new with a modern stone and stucco front that was next to an old building that reminded Rich of Kay's Ceramics in Lamar. The clock above the entrance to City Hall read 2:45. Just north of City Hall the Team picked up Route 180 west and headed out of town. It would have been cool to see where Grandpa had supper, but there was no record of that in his diary, and many of the stores along 191 and 180 looked far too modern to have been around 100 years ago.

Route 180 was flat with long stretches of straight roads. On either side of the road was barren land with hardly a tree in sight. The landscape consisted of short brown grass. Nothing seemed to grow more than two feet tall. An occasional cow or two was seen wandering in the grasses. Continuing on there was not a cloud in the sky. The flat horizon glowed as the sun started to set.

Heading toward the Petrified Forest

Before the dark had settled in the Team pulled off at the Petrified Forest Information Center in Holbrook, Arizona. The Team loaded the Maxwell on the trailer and performed their usual shutdown procedure of draining and replacing oils. It was a productive day for the Team. They logged 227 miles with the Maxwell with no roadside repairs or adjustments needed. After the Maxwell was tied down they then walked through the gift shop at the Petrified Forest and saw incredible polished tables, shelves, and decorations revealing an array of colorful polished petrified tree artifacts. Fascinating to look at but the boys left without loading any souvenirs into the Chevy.

It was dark, by the time they left the gift shop. They climbed into the Chevy van and headed back out on to Route 180 west. While in the Chevy they discussed the goal for the night. They looked for a place to stay in Flagstaff, but hotels were booked up. Apparently, unknown to the Team, this weekend was the annual Festival of Trees; hotels were sold out. They realized if they made it to Winslow that night, they would be able to get to the Walnut Canyon National Monument Park by noon. The cliff dwellings that Grandpa had visited were now part of that park. The Team was expecting to have another photo opportunity there.

They landed in Winslow around 7 PM. They checked in at the Best Western before leaving for downtown Winslow to see the infamous "Corner in Winslow Arizona" from the popular Eagles song.

A stop at that "Corner in Winslow Arizona"

After walking around the famous corner the Team looked for a place for dinner. The town was pretty quiet with not a lot of choices. It was not a bee hive of activity this time of year. They ended up eating at a Denny's on the way back to the Best Western. It was John's first experience with Denny's.

Once back at the hotel, a few loads of laundry were started. Rich got to work on posting the latest pictures and videos on the website to share the day's adventure. Reflecting on Grandpa's progress they realized how Grandpa started his day in Winslow but only made it as far as Flagstaff, Arizona. The reason was because Grandpa and Scull had to wait there for gasoline. Grandpa's lead went from 270 miles to a mere 60 miles.

CWT diary entry Day 11:

Sunday, November 26, 1916. Therm 30 Weather Fair

Got up by a scare as we didn't drain radiator. Luckily it wasn't cold. Went up to Grand Canyon. Some wonderful. Took pictures, car on point. Made 150 miles. Wrote to folks. Sent other cards Fine weather. Stopping at a small boarding house. Keep loosing things lately!

Team Maxwell Day 11:

Saturday, November 26, 2016. Therm 22 Weather cloudy

By 7:30 AM the Team was fed and had the Maxwell uncovered ready for an exciting new photo opportunity: the cliff dwellings Grandpa visited so long ago.

Ready to start day number 11

During the morning check out Doug noticed the driver's side fender mounting nut was loose. This allowed the front fender to rattle. It was the source of the noise Doug had noticed the previous day. Unfortunately, because the bolt was attached to the inside of the fender, it was not a simple matter of getting a wrench on it to tighten the nut and bolt combination. Instead, Doug used a piece of fuel line hose wedged between the fender and the mounting bracket. Another problem was solved, no more rattling.

After filling the Maxwell and Chevy with gas the Team left Winslow by 8:15 AM on their way to the cliff dwellings at the Walnut Canyon National Monument Park. It was about 50 miles away from Winslow. Unfortunately, a review of available roads revealed the need to travel Interstate 40 until the Walnut Canyon National Monument exit. The Saturday traffic was light this early in the morning so the ride was not bad. On Interstate 40 they saw the snow-covered mountains were ahead. As the road turned to the left and right those snow-covered mountains switched sides of the Interstate. Doug and Rich guessed that Flagstaff was at the base of those mountains. At just about 10 AM they reached exit 204, Walnut Canyon Road. They exited the interstate and headed south on Walnut Canyon road toward the park. The two-lane road with no shoulder was lined with trees and small shrubs. The road led right into the park where the Team stopped and headed towards the Park's Information Center.

Inside they met with Ranger Kyle Ackerman in a sharply pressed, short-sleeve, tan and green park ranger uniform with a straight brimmed ranger hat. Ranger Kyle presented a sharp contrast to the boys who sported multiple layers of warm clothes. He was one of the folks Rich had been in contact with prior to the visit. He provided a trail map and showed the Team the location of the dwelling identified in Grandpa's photograph. The dwelling was not on the trail but on the opposite side of the canyon. It was off limits to the public.

The Team walked down Island Trail into the park. It was a cardio workout. The narrow trail snaked down into the canyon, passing cliff dwellings along the way. Edges of the trail had sharp drops into the ravine which encouraged the boys to stay to the right as they made their way down. It was incredible imaging Indians used to live in these dwellings. When they reached the point on the trail where Grandpa's cliff dwelling could be observed, it was obvious why the dwelling was off limits. Looking across the canyon the Team could see how much of a challenge it would be even for a billy goat to scale the south side. Everyone wondered how Grandpa had ever gotten there.

A view of the Cliff Dwelling Grandpa visited in 1916

On the way out the Team thanked Ranger Kyle for his help. Everyone had theorized how Grandpa might have gotten to that dwelling, but Ranger Kyle explained the road the Team had used to come into the park was not there a hundred years ago. There was a dirt road open to traffic called Old Walnut Canyon Road which was more likely a road traveled by Grandpa. "We gotta drive on it" was Doug's response. After a few pictures with Ranger Kyle the Team left the park and headed for the old dirt road. Rich left behind golden rock #11.

The Team found the road Ranger Kyle mentioned. He was correct that it was a dirt road, a very primitive one at that! The road was filled with deep ruts; rocks and ice covered mud puddles. Tall pine trees stood along both sides with an old split-rail fence on the south side. It was only a mile or so in when the smooth dirt road turned into a wagon trail. The Maxwell bounced along slowly. Having a high ground clearance helped the Maxwell navigate the obstacles in the road. The mud puddles added a layer of dirt to everything. Rich was nearly bounced out of the Maxwell, but he was more concerned about John following in the Chevy pulling the trailer. It was a road best navigated by off-road vehicles. It was a real challenge to navigate the Chevy van with the trailer. Doug and Rich stopped at one point and waited for John to catch up. It was a thrill to drive on this road even though it was slow going. Grandpa must have used part of this road to get to the cliff dwellings on the south side of the canyon.

The Team followed the Old Walnut Canyon Road until they got to paved roads that led them towards Flagstaff and Historic Route 66. Their next photo opportunity would be at the Grand Canyon north of Flagstaff by way of Route 180. It was a 75 mile trek along Route 180, then Route 64 north to the south rim of the Grand Canyon.

Route 180 was a two-lane road that cut through a forest of tall pine trees. It was a 65 MPH road with a shoulder of gravel and grass, which presented a problem as cars gathered behind the Chevy with its flashers going. The road did have an occasional passing zone, but cars seemed to collect behind the Team quickly. There were not a lot of places to get off the road and driving on grass and gravel to let cars pass was not ideal. After about fifteen miles, Doug thought it would be a good idea to exit off of 180 on a side road to let cars pass. He turned onto Fire Road 794. The fire road was not well traveled but begged for adventure so Doug and Rich drove deeper into the woods while John waiting with the Chevy van along the highway. There was no telling once down this road if the Chevy with trailer in tow would be able to turn around. Along the road is where the Maxwell had its first encounter with snow.

The Maxwell drives through snow

While driving down the fire road a herd of Elk ran across the boys path a hundred yards ahead. Doug and Rich turned around in the snow and headed back to connect with John. The Team continued on towards the Grand Canyon.

Doug and John continued along Route 180 for another thirty-five miles then headed north on Route 64 while Rich followed in the Chevy. Since Rich had the luxury of a radio, he tuned into an interesting radio broadcast about Fred Harvey and his success with establishing the Harvey House chain of restaurants in 1878. These fine dining eating establishments were located at railroad stations and catered to rail travelers. The waitresses hired by Fred had to be between 18-30, single, attractive and intelligent. They also had strict guidelines on their behavior, hair style, could not use makeup, and had to wear starched black and white uniforms. They were called Harvey Girls. Rich mused over how times have changed. Little did Rich know this was not the last he would hear about the Harvey Girls.

They were still about thirty miles from the south rim of the Grand Canyon. These next thirty miles were as heart pounding as a roller-coaster ride; not because of hills or sudden drops in the road but because of the traffic on the two-lane highway. Route 64 is the only choice to take visitors to the south rim from Flagstaff. It was just two lanes with a gravel shoulder. The curves in the road meant there was only an occasional dotted yellow line for passing slower cars. The result was a long line of anxious cars behind a 35 MPH Maxwell. The Team did not experience any road rage, but what they did experience were drivers pushing the envelope when passing slower cars.

These anxious drivers waited for the dotted yellow line only to find oncoming traffic that prevented them from exercising their passing maneuver. When there was an opportunity, Doug moved the Maxwell to the right as much as possible, sometimes he rode the gravel shoulder, so there was more room to pass. Most cars passed safely but more than once, there were drivers who attempted to pass, with oncoming cars (doing 65 MPH) approaching. Rich who followed in the Chevy saw oncoming cars flashing their lights at the passing cars. One time the oncoming car had to run off the road on to the shoulder. The Team all later agreed that it was insane.

Once at the Grand Canyon Park, they realized they were probably visiting the canyon on one of the busiest days of the year. There were few parking spots for cars much less a Chevy van with a trailer. The Team loaded the Maxwell on the trailer right in the parking lot because no one wanted to drive the Maxwell back south on Route 64, plus with the Maxwell on the trailer they found a spot to park with the recreational motor homes.

The visit to the edge of the canyon was remarkable. The views were spectacular and the crowds were heavy. Doug and Rich posed for a picture and replicated the picture of Grandpa and Scull at the canyon one hundred years ago.

Two pictures separated by 100 years

Rich even pulled up his jeans to make his outfit look like Grandpa's high-water pants. Even John, (who was not a big fan of heights) gingerly approached the railing for a picture with the beautiful canyon behind him. After walking along the rim admiring the views the boys picked up some hot coffee at one of the snack bars and headed back to the Maxwell. It was getting close to 5 PM, time to move westward.

The drive south on Route 64 in the Chevy was much less stressful with the Maxwell on the trailer. While driving, the Team considered where they should spend the night. They wanted to meet Allan Borne and Nick Cataldo in San Bernardino by Monday around noon. If they made it to Kingman for the night, then they could experience the Route 66 drive to Oatman in the morning and get the within striking distance of San Bernardino for a noon arrival on

Monday. This sounded like a plan, so a room was booked at the Hampton Inn in Kingman while on the road, something Grandpa never would have been able to do.

Kingman was over a 150 miles away which meant the Team would be in the Chevy for just short of three hours. Not a long ride, except for the guy that was sitting in the middle seat. Once in Kingman, they grabbed a bite to eat at Kingman's Cracker Barrel Restaurant. It was the second time eating at a Cracker Barrel, but the food was good and the location convenient. Once in the hotel, the boys started a couple of loads of laundry and reviewed their progress. They had, in fact, passed Grandpa who spent another day in the Grand Canyon and Flagstaff region waiting for a gas delivery. One of the many luxuries the Team enjoyed over Grandpa's trip was the plethora of gas stations. Rich worked on posting a new blog entry to capture the day's events in pictures and videos. It was a memorable day.

CWT diary entry Day 12:

Monday, November 27, 1916. Therm 25 Weather Fine

Another day of waiting. Sent about 15 cards. Walked up to Lowell Observatory. Got watch fixed.

Team Maxwell Day 12:

Sunday, November 27, 2016. Therm 52 Weather windy

The morning ritual included a check of all the oil levels since it was not done in the Grand Canyon parking lot. The day started in the 40s with a stiff wind. As the day progressed, it did warm up into the 50s. The sun was out in full force with just a few scattered clouds. So it was another excellent day for a drive in the open-air Maxwell. The Team all knew how lucky they were to have such great weather for the trip so far, but no one spoke about it in fear of jinxing their good fortune. Especially since the morning weather reports were citing a storm coming in from the California coast.

Months prior, in preparing for the trip the Team learned about the old mining town called Oatman, a place mentioned in Grandpa's diary. It was a town on the original Route 66 and a popular attraction for those riding the Route 66 trail. Oatman began as a small mining camp shortly after two prospectors found a multi-million dollar gold mine in 1915, just a year before Grandpa's visit. The town's name was in honor to Olive Oatman. She was a young Illinois girl that had been taken captive by Indians when her pioneer family traveled westward. The Team also knew that burros often wandered the streets in Oatman. The Team was anxious to visit this town.

The Team filled the Maxwell and the Chevy up with gas for the day's start. It was 9:15 AM, or maybe 10:15 AM. The boys were amused over the fact their phones were giving different times. The phones appeared to be switching between Mountain Standard Time and Pacific Standard Time at the hotel. The Team concluded that it was 10 AM as the Maxwell left Kingman on Historic Route 66. As they were leaving town, the road paralleled the railroad tracks that was hosting a very long freight train also traveling west. For a short span of time, the Maxwell was able to keep up with the long train, but they soon parted ways when Doug and Rich crossed under Interstate 40 to pick up the Oatman Highway with John following in the Chevy.

It was a 23 mile drive on the Oatman Highway to get to downtown Oatman. The first 12 miles were nearly perfectly straight, flat two lane road with dirt shoulders. The highway had occasional dips in the road which appeared as if the road was crossing a dried river bed. Posted signs warned not to cross if the road if flooded. The surrounding landscape consisted of small patches of deer grass and short shrubs with no trees, and nothing taller than six feet. Straight ahead was the Black Mountain range. Blue skies and thin clouds laced over the top of the mountains. It was a spectacular view.

Oatman Highway towards the Black Mountains

Once at the foothills of the Black Mountains, the Oatman Highway took on a very different character. Instead of being straight and flat, it was narrow and winding as it snaked its way up and over the mountains. The Maxwell took on the hills in second and sometimes first gear. As the Team rose higher up the mountain, the road shoulders got steeper and scarier. There were no shoulder or guard rails. If the car had the misfortune of leaving the road, it would mean disaster. It was a road meant for a James Bond car chase scene. It was a fun road to drive on for the thrill seeker. It was filled with sharp blind curves and switch backs as it crept to the top of the mountain. Rich turned to Doug, "According to Grandpa's diary, he and Scull drove all night through mountains and Oatman, can you imagine driving on this road at night?" Both Doug and Rich reflected on how courageous Grandpa must have been. Then again, if it was dark maybe they did not realize how close they were to danger.

By 11:00 AM, the Maxwell had reached the top of Sitgreaves Pass, at an elevation of 3,550 feet. Doug pulled off the road into the dirt before starting the downhill ride. Like the mountains in Pennsylvania, it would mean using a lot of the lower gears to slow the Maxwell down. This was one time they did not want to go fast in the Maxwell. Unlike the mountains in Pennsylvania, there was very little protection in the form of guard rails. Doug and Rich decided that John, and the Chevy should lead the way down the Black Mountain to Oatman, just in case the Maxwell needed help stopping.

Over, and now down the Black Mountain

They reached Oatman without having to use the Chevy and trailer for an emergency stop. The town of Oatman was just like one would picture as a western mining town that was untouched by time. The Oatman Hotel, Oatman General Store, and the White Bird Trading Post with its old-style Texaco gas pumps, which probably arrived after Grandpa was there. This town had lots of character as the Team got out and strolled down Main Street just in time to catch a gun fight, a staged gun fight of course but authentic characters with loud revolvers.

The Team made a point to stop in at the White Bird Trading Post. Inside the trading post was an assortment of clothing, souvenirs, and the smell of leather. Towards the back of the post was the proprietor, Monica Kerr. Monica sat on a stool wearing a sweatshirt and woolly fingerless gloves.

A stop at the trading post in Oatman, Arizona

Monica was a delightful lady and told the boys to visit the Oatman Hotel where Clark Gable and Carole Lombard visited after their wedding in Kingman. Monica also told about her encounter with "Oatie" a legendary friendly poltergeist. Oatie is believed to be William Ray Flour, an Irish miner who died behind the hotel.

By 12:30 PM, the Team was back on the road destined for Needles, California their next stop. On the way out of Oatman, Doug and John stopped to see the famous wild burros that freely roam around the streets of Oatman.

The famous burrows of Oatman roam the streets

Doug and John headed west on Oatman road, which turned back into a nearly straight and flat two-lane road. As they did the clouds grew heavier and darker. It appeared as if the weather forecast was correct and a storm was headed in their direction. In fact, as they traveled US Highway 95 south towards Needles, the rain started. At first, it was a light drizzle but it quickly turned into a real downpour. Only the second time in twelve days that the Team had seen rain. The last time was back in Pennsylvania.

Doug and John pulled into a gas station with covered gas pumps. They would put the Maxwell top up under the protection of the covering, but they paused and thought about it for a few moments. Once they get into California, they will have to cross the Mojave Dessert. Surely it does not rain in the dessert. Or at least, they did not think it would rain. They decided not to put up the top and tough it out, drive through the storm towards drier Mojave Dessert weather.

The rain did stop as the Team crossed the Colorado River about an hour later. This was the same location where Grandpa used a ferry operated by the Mojave Indians. They celebrated entering California, state number twelve with lunch at Jack in the Box in Needles.

Leaving Needles meant the Team had to do some driving on Interstate 40 for 26 miles where they could pick up the National Trails Highway for more driving on side roads. Unfortunately, that exit was closed for, from what they could tell, was for some road work. So Doug and John continued across the Mojave National Preserve. It was flat and straight but not as hot for the Team, as Grandpa mentioned in his diary. Just the opposite, it started to rain again. The Team would later laugh about the fact they drove so far with no rain, the last spot they expected to hit rain would be on the Mojave Dessert portion of their trip. The rain did not last long, but the traffic was fast and being a slow-moving vehicle was not a fun drive. With no other side roads and the extremely fast moving traffic the Team decided for safety reasons they would load the Maxwell on the trailer. They had covered 120 miles.

Rich who was following in the Chevy had been in contact with Allen Bone in San Bernardino. Since it was the end of the Thanksgiving holiday weekend Allan's suggested stopping for the night before getting to the Cajon Pass where the traffic was likely to be heavy as folks visiting Las Vegas, Nevada would be returning. Allen's suggestion was to spend the night in Victorville and take on the Cajon Pass into San Bernardino in the morning.

With the Maxwell on the trailer, the Team picked a Hilton Garden Inn hotel in Victorville. That night the Team ate at Giuseppe's Restaurant. Then back to the hotel where Rich recorded the day in pictures and videos on the website while Doug and John relaxed. They reflected how poor Grandpa was still waiting for gasoline in order to continue his journey. For the first time, the Team was ahead of Grandpa, not because of their driving skill but because of the availability of gasoline.

CWT diary entry Day 13:

Tuesday, November 28, 1916. Therm 50 Weather Fine

Watchful waiting. We drove out to the prehistoric cliff dwellings today 1500 ft. to bottom of canyon. Took two pictures. Sent a letter to Helen card enclosed. Sent a card to folks.

Team Maxwell Day 13:

Monday, November 28, 2016. Therm 44 Weather sunny

This morning there was excitement in the air. The Team had made it to California; the Maxwell was running well with Los Angeles less than 100 miles away. This trip was clearly doable for the Maxwell. The weather was sunny and a comfortable 44 degrees to start with a promise of it getting warmer.

Rich had spoken with Nick Cataldo yesterday about the approach into San Bernardino from Victorville. Nick, an author with great knowledge of San Bernardino and the Cajon Pass suggested taking back roads to the Cajon Pass. The route included dirt roads. Mention driving on dirt roads and Doug was all in.

The Team was up and had the Maxwell uncovered before 8 AM. Rather than eating at the hotel this morning they decided on breakfast at an IHOP after loading up on gas. It was 9:30 AM by the time the Team was back on the road. Based on the suggestion from Nick, they traveled down Mariposa Road, which paralleled Interstate 15. It was just a two-lane road with a lot less traffic than the interstate. The Team could see the San Gabriel Mountains to the right and the San Bernardino Mountains to the left. Their route would take them between the two mountain ranges. The tops of the mountains were covered with snow. The sky was blue with wispy clouds on the horizon. It was going to be a good day.

They took Mariposa Road to the very end at which point the payment stopped and the dirt road began. It was Forest Route 3N45, an off-road vehicle delight, but for the Maxwell, it was another rut filled dirt road that nearly tossed Rich out of the Maxwell while doing a whopping 5 MPH. Much like the old entrance to the Walnut Canyon National Monument Park it was slow driving over the dirt road. Although it might not have been the exact road Grandpa traveled, all believe it represented the type of road he and Scull had to traverse. It was dusty, lumpy, and barren. Twice the road took them across railroad tracks with no lights or crossing gates. A careful pause was taken to be sure no train would suddenly appear from the curved track that disappeared around a corner. The ride was less than five miles but it was a very memorable one.

The "Forest Road" eventually connected up to the paved Route 138. Traveling west on 138 would take the Team through the Cajon Junction. The view towards the Cajon Pass was picturesque with two mountain ranges separated with a thin layer of clouds. The snow topped San Gabriel Mountains rising above the clouds.

Heading towards Cajon Pass

At Cajon Junction the Team had to get on Interstate 15 south but only for a mile and a half where they excited on to Cajon Boulevard, also called Historic Route 66. It was a straight shot into downtown San Bernardino. The Team pulled into the San Bernardino Metro Station by 11:30 AM. They waited at the metro station parking lot to join up with Allen Bone and Nick Cataldo. Doug connected up with A.J. Baime from the Wall Street Journal on the phone to give him a quick update.

Once the Team met Allen, and Nick, Allen gave the boys an absolutely fascinating tour of the San Bernardino History and Railroad Museum. Inside was old cars, old trains, and train station replicas. In a showcase was a life size manikin of a beautiful Harvey Girl, just like what Rich had heard about on the raido. Before the Team left the museum, Michel Nolan from the San Bernardino Sun stopped by to interview the Team about their adventure for a story she would be writing. After the interesting tour through the museum, and the interview, the Team was ready for the last leg of their trip.

Outside the San Bernardino Rail Station Museum

Los Angeles was only 60 miles away (one hour if you used a modern car on the interstate), but the Team was going to follow the historic Route 66 into Los Angeles with all its traffic lights. Allen advised it would likely take three hours. By 1:30 PM, the Team was on their way along Route 66 to Los Angeles. The drive was lined with shops, carefully pruned landscaping, palm trees, and traffic light after traffic light.

The drive along Route 66 was a nice ride but took longer than anticipated, and as they approached Los Angeles, the Maxwell starting running rough again. The last three days the Maxwell had been running like a top. But as the case with the older cars, they often required regular spark plug cleaning and point adjustments. Doug pulled off the road for a quick cleaning of the spark plugs but that alone did not solve the occasional misfire. The sun was setting, and the traffic was getting heavier. The Team wanted to get to downtown before dark, so they decided to continue driving the Maxwell even though it was running a little rough. The Team arrived at their final destination, the corner of Hope and Eleventh Street at 6 PM. This was the corner that once was the home to a Maxwell Motor Company sales office.

Waiting for them at Hope and Eleventh Street was their nephew Tim Takao and Doug's daughter Gabriella, who had recently relocated in Los Angeles to start a career in the film industry. People passing by asked about the Maxwell and the Team proudly shared their story. It did not seem like thirteen days had passed since the start of the adventure. It seemed like just yesterday they were leaving Newark, New Jersey. They had completed Doug's dream to celebrate Grandpa's accomplishment one hundred years ago. Rich dropped the last of the golden rocks, #12 on a piece of artificial grass there on the sidewalk.

Arrived in Los Angeles

After the celebrating and picture taking, the Maxwell was loaded up on the trailer. Tim's wife, Cristina and her family, Steve and Julie Post took the Team out for a celebratory dinner at Philippe's. It was an evening of laughter and celebration.

Chapter 5 – The Epilogue

The following day the Team relaxed in Los Angeles with a visit to the San Monica fishing pier followed by an afternoon of repairs on Gabriella's Mustang. With all the tools in the Chevy van the Team was able to change the oil and replace the brakes for Gabriella. Once finished it was time to look towards the trip back east. Unlike Grandpa though, it would be with the Maxwell on the trailer. That evening they headed out of Los Angeles and decided to spend the night at a Holiday Inn in Hesperia, California on the east side of the Cajon Pass before the big push back east.

By 8 AM the following morning the Team was on the road for the return trek back to New York. This trip was all on interstates starting with Interstate 40. They rotated drivers each undertaking a four hour shift. They drove for almost forty hours before stopping at a Holiday Inn in Terra Haute, Indiana for a much needed rest and shower. The Google maps said they were just twelve hours from home but that was only if you averaged 75 MPH and did not stop for food. It took closer to twenty hours. Doug and Rich dropped John off in Massapequa and arrived back at Doug's house in Aquebogue at 7 AM, tired and exhausted.

The Team had completed Doug's dream that was born eight years ago. In the process they grew to have a much deeper respect for their Grandfather. Making this trip one hundred years ago was quite the accomplishment. Having the opportunity to recreate the trip only made the boys appreciate just how much of a challenge it was, especially having been undertaken without many of the modern conveniences. For the most part, the Team had all paved roads, plenty of gas stations, places to eat and a hot shower every morning. But there were more observations made along the way like the number of times today's roads cross over creeks and valleys. One of the most common comments you would have heard if you were sitting in the back of the Maxwell was "How did Grandpa manage this?" C.W. Tuthill and P.G. Scull were men of men. Did the team ever catch up to Grandpa and Scull? Yes, but it was not a level playing field by any means.

Grandpa's adventure of course continued on after visiting San Francisco and San Diego. He and Scull made the return trip back east following a southern route through Texas and other southeastern states arriving back in Newark on January 25th. But their claim to fame was making the western leg of the trip in ten days and sixteen hours. Multiple newspapers around the country wrote about their accomplishment.

As far as what ever happen to that Maxwell, Rich found two articles written by Texaco describing in much detail the disassembly of the Maxwell engine and suspension for inspection of wear. Texaco was showcasing the quality of their lubricants with detailed descriptions and photos showing how well the engine parts held up over this grueling trip. One can only suspect that the car was never put back together or perhaps it was used for parts after that. What a shame.

In the months following the completion of the adventure Doug and Rich thought about the cliff dwellings at the Walnut Canyon National Monument and how it would have been fun if they would have been able to stand in the same spot Grandpa stood in his picture at the dwelling. Rich reached back out to the National Park Service and found out a special permit could be requested to have a ranger lead a hike to that location. However it would require approval from the National Park Services which does not come easily. Working with Ranger Mike Haubert, Rich filed the necessary paperwork and the request was approved.

Arrangements were made, and Doug and Rich returned to the Walnut Canyon National Monument in May 2017. Led by Ranger Mike, the three hiked down through the canyon valley and scaled back up the other side to the exact spot Grandpa had visited in November of 1916. The boys posed like Grandpa for pictures before returning back to the Visitor Center.

Grandpa at a cliff dwelling in 1916, Rich in 2017

It was a thrill to revisit the exact same spot as Grandpa stood. The boys were grateful for the support of Ranger Mike and the National Parks Service.

Reflecting on this adventure the Team realized how much they had to be grateful for. The weather might have been cold, but it was sunny most of the way. When things broke down a solution was always found to allow them to continue. It was truly a Team Maxwell effort that would not have happened without all the support from family and friends in the form of funds, technical expertise, their personal time, loaning us parts, and encouraging the chase of this dream. It was an adventure of a lifetime. Finally, Doug, Rich, and John want to send a "shout out" to Grandpa from the bottom of their hearts, "Thank you Grandpa" for watching over us.

Author contact information:

If you would like to contact the author, email Rich at: rbassemir1@gmail.com

For those interested in seeing additional pictures taken on the trip along with videos, read the daily blog posting that were done at the end of each day. They were called the Maxwell chronicles and can be found at:

http://rtbassemir.com/1916-transcontinental-road-trip/2016-road-trip-story/the-maxwell-chronicles/

53462780R00082

Made in the USA
San Bernardino, CA
17 September 2017